A Pastor's Journal

Catholic Parishes and Schools Working Together

James T. Mulligan, CSC

NOVALIS

Cover design: Martin Gould
Layout: Audrey Wells

Published by Novalis

Publishing Office
10 Lower Spadina Avenue, Suite 400
Toronto, Ontario, Canada
M5V 2Z2

Head Office
4475 Frontenac Street
Montréal, Québec, Canada
H2H 2S2

www.novalis.ca

Library and Archives Canada Cataloguing in Publication

Mulligan, James T. (James Terrance), 1942-, author
A pastor's journal : parishes and schools working together
/ James T. Mulligan, CSC.

Issued in print and electronic formats.
ISBN 978-2-89688-136-9 (pbk.).--ISBN 978-2-89688-137-6 (mobi).--
ISBN 978-2-89688-138-3 (epub).--ISBN 978-2-89688-139-0 (pdf)

1. Catholic Church--Education--Canada. 2. Catholic schools--Canada. I. Title.

LC504.M86 2015 371.071'271 C2014-908474-9
C2014-908475-7

Printed in Canada.

We acknowledge the financial support of the Government of Canada through the Canada Book Fund for business development activities.

5 4 3 2 1 19 18 17 16 15

CONTENTS

Acknowledgements

I wish to thank those who have contributed in one way or another to this book. As the book records the life of a parish, I must thank first of all my Holy Cross confrere, Father Vijay Amirtharaj, who is now pastor of the Parish Community of St. Kevin. Father Vijay and I are closely involved in pastoral collaboration with our four Catholic schools. His humour, work ethic and social awareness are prized pastoral characteristics in ministry and in service to the Catholic education project. Marney Donohue is our super-capable administrative assistant. She is the keeper of the *Green Binder*, the communicator with principals and teachers, the provider of the necessary canonical forms and catechetical materials, and the coach, supportive of and strategizing for parents, teachers and priests. Marney makes it easy and indeed joyful to minister here at St. Kevin's. I also wish to recognize Diana Lopez Marin and thank her for her role in keeping our parish team nourished and refreshed.

I would like to recognize the generosity and gifts of many of the teachers in our parish schools, and thank them and their principals for their lived commitment to Catholic education. I also want to thank in a special way my long-time friend and colleague Therese Parent. As I kept this journal over the ten months of the school year, Therese has been a constant and deeply appreciated source of encouragement and a gentle but firm guardian of language and syntax. Her insights and suggestions were very helpful in shaping this text.

Finally, I take this opportunity to publicly recognize and thank the hundreds of Catholic educators across Canada who, in their teaching and witnessing, live out their baptismal priesthood. Catholic education will survive and indeed thrive as long as a significant number of Catholic teachers see their work as a special vocation grounded in their Baptism and serving the mission of the church. May many other teachers in our Catholic schools be inspired by the convictions and lived faith of these faithful women and men.

As I review the pages of this book and see the text as a whole, I am a little surprised but very pleased by the different references to the baptismal priesthood and lay ministry, to social justice and to "collegiality" as experienced through lived community and collaboration. These, I believe, are clear characteristics of the teaching and spirit of the Second Vatican Council. I am very much taken, too, with the voice of Pope Francis that is heard in the text through his Apostolic Exhortation *On the Joy of the Gospel.* Pope Francis, I feel, has given new vision and inspiration to the evangelizing project – an inspiration and vision very much grounded in the teaching and spirit of the Second Vatican Council. And when I think of the Second Vatican Council I think of Bishop John O'Mara, a friend and mentor, who in November 2014 celebrated his 90th birthday. Bishop O'Mara is Bishop Emeritus of the Diocese of St. Catharines. I greatly value my years of ministering collaboratively with Bishop O'Mara, a priest and bishop profoundly formed by the Second Vatican Council. To Bishop O'Mara I dedicate this book.

James T. Mulligan, CSC
January 2015

PART I

RECORDING THE GIFTS AND CHALLENGES

A YEAR IN THE RELATIONSHIP OF PARISH AND CATHOLIC SCHOOL

INTRODUCTION

Why This Journal?

When it comes to our relationship with our Catholic schools, I think we have a good thing going here in the Parish Community of St. Kevin. Is it the best possible arrangement? Not at all! But we work at it. We serve four Catholic schools in the parish: three elementary schools and one high school. I started this journal for my own purposes: to understand more and to see how parish and school structurally might have more depth and quality in transmitting the faith. I thought that it would be useful to keep a record of our collaboration with our schools—useful for us as we review our evangelizing mission and useful for the principal, staff and school when they reflect on their own mission. Thus this journal!

As well, I have a certain bias for Catholic education. I am a Holy Cross Father. We are formed in the spirit of our charism *to educate in the faith.* My ministry since ordination has been to serve as a Catholic educator: as a classroom teacher, chaplain, curriculum coordinator and faith-formation animator. So nine years ago, in assuming the ministry of pastor here at St. Kevin's, it was natural for me to be particularly sensitive to what goes on in our Catholic schools and to the existing relationship between parish and school. This journal helps me to give an account of how I have lived out my bias for Catholic education in my years as pastor.

This journal is based on a particular school year (2013–2014), and includes references to events that were current at the time. Although I speak of specific events in that year, feel free to think of a more recent relevant event in the news or in the church. There are always current events that prompt a conversation about our faith.

The Catholic Education Project

Over the years, I have reflected on the Catholic education project and how vital it can be for the local church. Local church, for my purposes, is both diocese and parish. My theology of Catholic education—as well as being grounded in our Holy Cross charism of *educating in the faith*—is rooted in church teaching:

> The Catholic school finds its true justification in the mission of the Church; it is based on an educational philosophy in which faith, culture and life are brought into harmony. Through it the local Church evangelizes, educates, and contributes to the formation of a healthy and morally sound life-style among its members. (*The Religious Dimension of Education in a Catholic School* [1988], 34)

I am convinced that Catholic education is very much a part of, and vital to, the mission of the church. In concrete terms, that means vital for a parish blessed enough to have a Catholic school. And I feel that we are singularly blessed to have the Catholic education network we have in the provinces of Ontario, Alberta and Saskatchewan. We have a fully funded Catholic education system and many excellent Catholic educators; this funding and such a plurality of Catholic teachers is something that struggling jurisdictions can only dream of. As a pastor, I experience first-hand the great social and faith capital the Catholic school can be for the parish.

In this journal, I describe some possibilities for evangelizing the young Catholics in our care—young Catholics who represent the future adult church. This is the gift Catholic education offers to the church.

In my earlier writing, I chose to reflect on something that I was a part of and vitally involved in as teacher and as a faith formator. Now, as a pastor, I see the Catholic education project from a new angle. And as a pastor with responsibility for sacramental preparation, I am working with the children in our schools and encountering the parents of these children. Even at this stage of my life, I find that the children teach me. I continue to learn, as well, from those parents and about those parents; that means I am acquiring a new understanding of different aspects of the present and future of our church community. The contemporary Catholic school continues to serve as the canary in the coal mine for the present and future life of Catholic education and, in a way, for the church as well.

The Value of Sunday Eucharist

As a pastor, I live Sunday Eucharist, the day of the Lord. At the same time, I can't help but reflect on the irregular participation or even absence of many Catholic parents and Catholic educators from this weekly celebration. As a pastor, I see the shape of the church being formed now in the students in our schools. This means two things. There are some very wonderful and committed young people who will grow in their faith and appreciation of the importance of the church for living their lives. But at the same time, many good young people are like their parents, and active participation in church is not a great priority. It seems that faith is present in their lives, but it is a faith that needs a great amount of "rekindling" or "fanning into a flame" (2 Timothy 1:6). This is the continuing challenge coming through Catholic education to the Catholic school and to the local church.

There are several elements to the working theology in our parish's collaboration with the Catholic school:

- We have a very happy and positive appreciation of the great gift that the Catholic school and Catholic education are for the church of Ontario.
- We reverence the baptismal priesthood and ministry of the laity and the many gifts of countless Catholic teachers.

- We look at the teacher in the Catholic school as having *a vocation* and the Catholic school itself as having *a mission*—vocation and mission that must be grounded intimately in knowledge of and friendship with Jesus.
- We proceed from an ecclesiology that is both welcoming and hospitable, and we want to be a church that is not closed but wants to serve all of the baptized, no matter their present relationship with the church and the parish.
- We realize that our social and cultural context has dramatically changed and continues to change, and that the deep secularization we are working in calls for new and creative ways of transmitting the faith. This is what is called the new evangelization.
- We are well aware that there is always the risk of mediocrity, both in some of the teachers and administrators in the schools and in our own performance as a parish team.

The New Evangelization: Building on "Slivers" of Faith

"Just because he had lost track of his faith didn't mean that it had left him." This is an observation on the part of the narrator in Olen Steinhauer's novel *The Cairo Affair*. The Egyptian intelligence chief has invited his young partner to his apartment for supper. After supper, the young agent says that he is going to pray. His chief says that he, too, will pray. And the narrator writes, "Just because he had lost track of his faith didn't mean that it had left him." This is but a glimpse into the soul of a secular Muslim who had lost track of his faith. I think the same thing can be said of many Catholics today. On several occasions in this journal, I referred to faith, even a sliver of faith, that is somehow present in a parent who brings her child to one of our schools or to a teacher who has become very secularized. With so many secular distractions, Catholic believers can easily lose track of their faith. The faith option becomes exactly that—an option among so many other options. But I think faith does remain an option. That sliver of faith is grace: the loving presence of a resilient God who does not abandon us. Furthermore, I see that sliver of faith as being a stepping stone and an opportunity to be present to secular Catholics in the Catholic education world, to invite them to claim more ownership of the faith that is theirs, to discover its richness and meaning, and to assure them of the hospitality that awaits them in the parish and at Sunday Eucharist.

Finding a Balance: Parish and School

As a priest and as a Catholic educator, I find myself in a unique and privileged position. One might say that I hear it from both sides! On the one hand, there are times when I have to listen to some priests go on and on:

- Our schools are Catholic in name only, and nothing of substance happens in the Catholic school.
- The children do not know doctrine, and they don't come to church.
- Worse still, their teachers don't come to church.
- The principal is not at all open to discussing with the staff the Catholic character of the school or providing any type of faith formation for the teachers.

On the other hand, I have also been privy to some of the disappointments Catholic educators have experienced with the parish:

- Father's approach is very authoritarian.
- Father has a great deal of difficulty relating and speaking to the children.
- Our priest seems to want to take the church back to the times before Vatican II.
- Because of language difficulties, nobody understands what Father is saying.

There is negativity, but there is so much more positivity! I have come to hear about many schools and parishes that have great admiration for one another: principals and parish priests work beautifully together, priests are very present in the Catholic school, and teachers are entrusted by the parish with the sacred ministry of helping prepare children for the sacraments. Some exciting things are taking place in the handing on of our faith.

While the writing here is personal and meant to help us in-house, perhaps in a way this journal as a record of one school year might serve as a how-to guide or at least as a collection of resources for evangelization. So far, our situation here at St. Kevin's borders on the ideal. We are blessed. We are two Holy Cross Fathers with a supportive and experienced administrative assistant and a small group of lay ministers to depend on. It helps, too, that on occasion (such as for the sacrament of Reconciliation), we can draw on two or three of our Holy Cross Fathers living at our Centre House close by. We know that parishes with only one priest live a whole different reality. What I am proposing in these pages is simply one approach to evangelization.

Evangelizing in a postmodern culture calls for creative flexibility. For sure, in a one-priest parish, a few lay ministers sharing collaboratively in the ministry would be a great help. Many one- or two-priest parishes are connecting with Catholic schools and doing some rich evangelizing and faith formation with Catholic families. While we collaborate with four schools, we are aware that in some places, especially in the Greater Toronto Area, a parish may be connected to twice that number of schools. Again, it comes down to that creative flexibility.

We Can't Take Catholic Education for Granted

I must underscore the great contemporary urgency facing the Catholic community, schools and parishes—an urgency that manifests itself in three distinct ways:

- The urgency inherent in the content of the gospel and the message of the Good News of our Lord and Saviour, Jesus Christ.
- The urgency for parish communities to reach out in a welcoming, healing way to all Catholics.
- The urgency for the Catholic school and Catholic educators to deepen their commitment and embrace more joyfully the mission of the Catholic school.

To take our situation for granted is the sin that crosses borders of every sort. It is the sin that diminishes and compromises the urgency—taking for granted God's blessings; taking for granted the love that enriches our life daily; taking for granted that there will always be time. And so on. This taking for granted applies very much to the Catholic school and Catholic education as a vital dimension of the mission of the church.

It is really dumb on our part, on the part of all of the partners in Catholic education, to take Catholic education for granted. (My definition of "dumb" is "naively careless"). Catholic education is an enduring gift, but it is a fragile one. We have the lesson of Newfoundland and Labrador, a province that lost fully funded Catholic education. It would be dumb for teachers to think that their jobs and their schools are always going to be there. The schools and jobs will not endure unless teachers are working hard now and making sacrifices, living their teaching not as a job but as a vocation, as an extension of their Baptism. It would be dumb for parents to depend on the Catholic school to teach their kids religion now without investing themselves through interest, volunteering and participating in the life of the Catholic school community. It would be dumb for a parish to ignore or fail to see the evangelizing potential that the Catholic school offers. It would be dumb to overlook the possibility of missionary outreach to the non-engaged Catholics in the geography of the parish.

Embracing Our Mission

In conversations about ministry these last few years, I have often heard the Catholic school described as "missionary territory." I think this idea of missionary territory has to do with our current context—a context of increasing secularization. Our schools have great numbers of non-Catholic and occasional-Catholic students. The sense we have attached to "missionary" is that doing Catholic education is very hard and lonely, leaving us uncertain and fearful. It is almost as though we have reached the final stage before the disappearance of Catholic education altogether. And then along comes Pope Francis to give us a renewed and joyful understanding of "mission" and "missionary."

The leadership of Pope Francis is surely a special moment of grace for the post–Vatican II church. In the very first sentences of his Apostolic Exhortation *The Joy of the Gospel* (*Evangelii Gaudium*), published on November 24, 2013, Pope Francis dispels the doom and gloom and fearfulness of what might have been our approach to mission:

> The joy of the gospel fills the hearts and lives of all who encounter Jesus. Those who accept his offer of salvation are set free from sin, sorrow, inner emptiness and loneliness. With Christ joy is constantly born anew. In this Exhortation I wish to encourage the Christian faithful to embark upon a new chapter of evangelization marked by this joy, while pointing out new paths for the Church's journey in years to come. (*The Joy of the Gospel,* 1)

It has been said that *The Joy of the Gospel* is Pope Francis' mission statement for the church. If so, then it can also be a wellspring for renewal and enrichment for the parish and the Catholic school—indeed, for all partners in Catholic education—as we discern new paths for our journey now and in the years to come. The pope's words can inspire and support us as we begin to understand ourselves as missionary disciples, and our work in Catholic education as missionary activity.

I welcome Pope Francis as a companion as I make my way through this journal. Honouring his voice, his conviction and his teaching, I share different selections of his exhortation that speak to me and to all evangelizing agents in our parish and Catholic school ministry.

The *Green Binder*

Before we begin, let me explain the *Green Binder.* The *Green Binder* is the source of our work together and becomes our guide in working together—parish and Catholic school. (We call it the *Green Binder* simply because the colour of the binder is green!) In the *Green Binder* we find the outline for all of the points of contact between the Catholic school and the parish from the end of August to the end of June. This planning was done during the principals' meeting that we hosted at the parish last June, before the end of the school year. The planning is detailed. Here's what the *Green Binder* includes:

September to December

- the outline of events and experiences with the agreed-upon dates and times
- a letter of encouragement and gratitude to the principal from the parish team
- a letter to Catholic educators, welcoming them back to the school and thanking them for their evangelizing ministry as Catholic educators and for their contribution to our evangelizing project here at St. Kevin's. (The principal sees to the distribution of this letter.)
- a letter to parents, all of whom (the Catholics, that is) are members of the Parish Community of St. Kevin. This letter emphasizes that we are blessed to have a Catholic school, the parish is here for them, and we look forward to journeying with them in the education of their children. The letter is sent home with the children during the first week of school.
- a reminder to establish times early on for meetings with First Communion teachers and Confirmation teachers to prepare the evangelizing strategy for us to work together with parents and students
- Mass texts for opening school Masses
- instructions for installing teachers in the ministry of distributing Holy Communion

- outline and dates for First Communion meetings with parents. The first 90-minute meeting is held at the church at the end of September. The second 90-minute meeting happens at the end of November.
- a reminder to establish an RCIC (Rite of Christian Initiation for Children) program for children (usually in Grade 2) who are not baptized but whose parents—at least one of them a Catholic—now would like them to be baptized and prepared for First Communion
- a letter to parents containing an invitation to be present for the distribution of rosaries to Grade 3 children at Sunday Mass in October, the month of the Rosary
- a letter to parents containing an invitation to be present for the distribution of New Testaments to Grade 4 children at a Sunday Mass at the end of October
- Mass texts for the Thanksgiving Mass at the church
- text for the Rite of Enrolment for Confirmation to take place during the one-day Confirmation retreat at the parish in late September
- text for the Confirmation Rite of Commitment to take place at the schools at the end of October
- texts for the sacrament of Confirmation that takes place in mid-November, and texts for the preparation, rehearsal and the sacrament of Reconciliation for the Confirmation candidates, which takes place the day before the Confirmation celebration
- the details for the sacrament of Reconciliation that happens at the church in early Advent for grade 4 to 8 students, and at the high school for secondary students
- the Rite of Inscription for First Communion children and their parents that takes place in late November at Sunday Mass
- the texts for the Advent-Christmas Mass celebrated at the church for students at the elementary schools and at the high school for the secondary students

January to June

- February 3 – Feast of St. Blaise and blessing of throats / Blessing formula and scripture readings
- letter to parents of Grade 3s about meeting at the church for faith formation regarding the Sacrament of Reconciliation
- Ash Wednesday and distribution of ashes – Mass at the schools / Mass readings and procedures for Mass in the gym
- letter to parents of Grade 2 children about the retreat in preparation for First Eucharist
- Palm Sunday THINKfast
- invitation to Grade 7 teachers regarding Holy Week Stations of the Cross for students
- letter to parents explaining the procedure for Easter Sunday First Communion with the family
- school Eucharist in Easter week at church – Mass readings
- letter explaining formal (class) First Communion
- process for Grade 3 first formal Reconciliation at church
- letter to parents inviting them to consider the request for Confirmation and outlining the process for Confirmation
- outline of the liturgy for the Confirmation Rite of Acceptance
- readings for the final Mass of the school year
- outline for the Graduation Mass for the Grade 8s
- date to meet with principals to plan September to December of the next school year

Though the *Green Binder* is an organizational tool, it ultimately is all about bringing the child and the Catholic school community to encounter Jesus. It is filled with strategies for faith education and sacramental preparation agreed upon by parish and school, and it outlines the initiatives that we take in the parish and the support and assistance we receive from the school, the principals and the teachers.

Note: Many of these documents are available for download to purchasers of this book. Visit novalis.ca/greenbinder.

AUGUST–DECEMBER

AUGUST 29

The End of Summer

This morning, I make a brief visit to the four Catholic schools in the parish. Three are elementary schools of about 375 students each, and the fourth is a high school with 1,300 students. I make sure to meet with each principal. We chat about the summer and their hopes for the coming school year. In some schools, summer construction or renovations are finishing up and we tour the sites. Before I leave, I give the principal the updated version of the *Green Binder.*

SEPTEMBER 4

Meeting with the Director of Religious Education for the Diocese

Sister Mary Kay drops by. She is working on Guidelines for the Reception of the Sacraments for the diocese. We spend a long hour going over our program, the mechanics of our working relationship with the parents, meetings, expectations and resources, and the roles of parish and school. I then outline for her the theology of why we do what we do. At least, I underline for her some fundamental principles: the understanding of church as a welcoming community versus an elitist excluding community, the primacy of Baptism and the priesthood of the baptized.

The reality is that most of the students in our Catholic schools are children of parents who are occasional Catholics; they are not as churched as Catholics were even 25 years ago. This means that the Catholic school, rather than the home, is primarily responsible for the faith formation and catechesis the children receive. It may be naïve and simplistic on my part, but I believe that somehow each student in the Catholic school is there because of grace. Sure, the discipline and the sports and the academics and the proximity of home to the Catholic school all play an important part, but for the baptized children, I believe that God's grace is at work here, and that is why they are with us. This means that school and parish have to do all we can when so little religious education seems to happen at home.

SEPTEMBER 5

Meeting with Grade 8 Teachers about the Students Preparing for the Sacrament of Confirmation

Confirmation is celebrated in the middle of November, before Advent. By this point in September, the formation program with the candidates is well under way. We began the process last May, when we met with the candidates and their parents. The school provides us with a contact point to reach those involved. The May meeting at the parish launched the formation/catechesis element and allowed us to outline the process we would follow over the next six months.

In meeting now with the Grade 8 teachers, we can review the process. Usually in September there is a new teacher who must be filled in on what will take place. We give them the date for the Confirmation retreat and the Rite of Enrolment; we agree on the Rite of Commitment that we will use in the schools; and we discuss possibilities for community service.

September 6

Communication with the Principals

Pope Francis calls for prayer for peace in Syria. This is a teachable moment for the school communities.

September 10

The Opening School Mass at the High School

The local Catholic high school was founded by our religious community, the Holy Cross Fathers. Even in the last decade or so, when Holy Cross religious have not been attached to the school, there remains a very close relationship between the school and our religious community. The school serves the families of eight parishes and some 1,300 students. Our parish is by far the largest of the group, accounting for 50 percent of the students. Since the school is within the parish boundaries, we have been given pastoral responsibility for the school community. Over the years, we have established a very good relationship with the administration of the school and with the chaplaincy and religious education departments. In our pastoral animation, my confrere, Father Vijay, has been doing sacramental ministry at the high school for the last two years. As he is away, I am pleased to have the opportunity to connect again with the high school community.

The school Mass is held in the gym. Bleachers are pulled out and chairs are set up. Because of the numbers, we have two Masses. This certainly makes it more manageable when it comes to keeping students' attention and ensuring behaviour appropriate for the Eucharist. It is always a challenge, however. These are the children of a culture that seems increasingly deaf and blind to the sacred. Their parents, for the most part, are occasional Catholics who have not been deeply socialized into Catholic practices and traditions. And, as elsewhere in Catholic education in Ontario, some of the students are not Catholic and even not Christian. The chaplaincy department prepares the servers and the readers. The music department provides the choir and musicians. Teachers are placed strategically in the gym. Their presence is meant to ensure calm and encourage attention.

The homily on this occasion is more catechetical. The school is named after Our Blessed Mother, *Notre Dame*. This is a good moment to tell the story of the beginning of the school, which becomes a moment to tell the story of Mary, the Mother of God. The opening school Mass is the time to bless and install those teachers who will serve as Communion Ministers for the school year. It is also the time to bless and commission the Student Council and members of the Social Climate Committee. (The Social Climate Committee is a very active group of students who work at maintaining the social environment of the school within the tradition of Catholic social teaching and gospel values.)

SEPTEMBER 11

Meeting with Grade 2 Teachers and Principals about First Communion

We count on the teachers to be our conduit with the parents and to help us organize the First Communion process in the parish. Through the parish bulletin, we have invited children who are not in our Catholic schools to participate in the First Communion program held at another city parish. There are usually two or three children in public schools whose parents want them to take part in our parish program. The meeting with the teachers gives us an overview of the key moments of preparation leading up to Easter Sunday.

SEPTEMBER 12

The Opening School Mass for Elementary Schools

In the parish, we have three elementary schools with about 375 students per school. Two of the schools are at a distance from the church. The third school is within a ten-minute walk. The school board is very generous, assuring bus transportation each time we have a celebration in the church. We have several such celebrations through the course of the school year. In the second week of September, each school community will come one morning for the opening school Mass. This involves students from junior kindergarten or ECKP (Early Childhood Kindergarten Program) up to Grade 8. In attendance, too, are some parents and grandparents. The routine is well established. Children leave the bus and make their way into the church. A teacher guides the students to the holy water font. The students bless themselves and then walk down the aisle to their section. Another teacher helps the students with the genuflection. The very little children come into the church holding the hand of an older student, their buddy.

The partnership is evident today. Teachers have been very responsible in preparing the readers and the Prayers of the Faithful. The readings are contained in the *Green Binder*. Each school creates its own prayers. Usually, a particular class is given the responsibility for furnishing the readers and creating the prayers. When we begin, a student reads an introduction to the Mass. The parish provides two music ministers; each school has its own choir.

The homily is always brief. A story works best, but the application must be clear. Having something for students to look at, such as a banner, the Stations of the Cross, the baptismal font, etc., also helps. Something visual absorbs their attention, if only for a minute.

After the homily, we commission several teachers who will serve as Communion Ministers. These teachers have been carefully selected and called. Some teachers seem to own their vocation as Catholic educators more seriously and more joyfully than others. One picks this up in conversations and classroom visits and from watching them connect with students. Such teachers are very present in their parishes. The principals have invited these teachers to serve as Communion Ministers. The teachers receive resources to help them deepen their own understanding of the Eucharist and to give them an appreciation of their ministry.

I watch the children exit the buses and parade into the church. This year the school board has instituted a school dress code across its jurisdiction. Perhaps I am too nostalgic, but I find that the uniformity makes for more order and more attention.

September 24

Meeting with Parents of Students Preparing for First Communion

Our First Communion program is established on the principle that the parents are the primary faith educators of their children. So our expectation is that the parents prepare their children for First Communion. And yet, most of our parents do not participate in Sunday Eucharist often; for them, church and parish, while important, are not the highest priority. So the parish tries to support them in this role. The Catholic school also plays a key part: we are blessed many times over in Ontario with a fully financed public Catholic school system, including a full religion curriculum and some extraordinary Catholic educators. The Catholic school is a vital part of the capital of a Catholic parish community.

The parish serves as the faith resource for parents throughout the year. In September, at the end of November and in February, we offer parent faith-formation sessions to form them on the meaning of the Eucharist and Sunday Mass, equip them with catechetical resources to journey with their children, and encourage them through conversation and sharing to embrace the holy task of preparing their children. We furnish each family with the same catechetical resource for First Communion (*We Share in the Eucharist*, Novalis, 2009) that the teachers will use in class with the children. Inevitably, we meet a certain resistance from a few parents. Some of the resistance is vocal; some is non-verbal, but can easily be read. *Why do we have to spend time coming for this? What are our Catholic schools for? Isn't this just another school or class event?* For a few, the resistance will dissipate over the course of our three sessions. Unfortunately, another few will continue to begrudge the time spent in the church as learners or students being trained and equipped to journey with their children.

September 25

Confirmation Retreat

The candidates for Confirmation come to the church hall for a day. Gary Bowron, a friend, parishioner and long-time religious educator, now retired, animates the retreat day. Several high school students, graduates of the Confirmation candidates' elementary school, assist him. The Pentecost story in Acts is the foundation for the sharing and reflection that take place. Over the course of the day, candidates explore the fruits and the gifts of the Holy Spirit through group conversation and skits. The high school students are very helpful as group leaders.

The day concludes with catechesis on the sacrament of Confirmation and the Rite of Enrolment that takes place in a prayer service upstairs in the church. Teachers representing the parish community present the candidates for the sacrament. Candidates renew their baptismal promises and then come forward, reverently touch the Easter (Paschal) candle and then sign their names in our parish *Book of the Sacraments.*

Reluctantly, we have moved the Rite of Enrolment from a Sunday Mass to the Confirmation Retreat. As in most parishes, most of our candidates and their families are irregular participants at Sunday Eucharist. Only a small minority would be present for the Rite of Enrolment when held at Sunday Mass. We give real importance to the Rite of Enrolment. Having it during the Confirmation retreat allows the candidates to deepen their understanding of the journey towards Confirmation.

September 29

Blessing and Distribution of Rosaries to Children in Grade 3

At Sunday Mass, our Grade 3 students each receive a rosary. With the help of a letter home to the family and the encouragement of the teacher, many of the Grade 3 students and their families from our three elementary schools participate in this ritual, which takes place after the homily. The Knights of Columbus provide the rosaries. There is a brief explanation on the meaning of the Rosary and on Mary, Jesus' mother. As it is the month of October, the month of the Rosary, parents and the assembly are encouraged to pray the Rosary on their own and as a family. The children then come forth and, with the teachers' help, the priest-celebrant gives a rosary to each student.

OCTOBER 3

A Year of Faith Highlight

Since Advent of 2012, the diocese, with the whole church, has been celebrating in different ways the Year of Faith. The Social Justice Committee in our parish thought that during this Year of Faith there should be emphasis on the faith that does justice. With that focus in mind, we invited Professor Mark McGowan of the University of St. Michael's College, University of Toronto, to spend a day with us. Professor McGowan prepared a presentation for the evening in the parish on *The Year of Faith and Catholic Social Teaching*. But since he has done considerable animation with Catholic teachers and administrators, we arranged for him to address the senior administration and principals of our local Catholic school board in the morning. As he is a historian specializing in the historical evolution of the Catholic community in Ontario, he gave a brilliant presentation on the struggle to establish, maintain and eventually grow Catholic education in the province. Knowing its history gives even more urgency to the holy task of safeguarding the enduring gift that is ours in Catholic education.

Taking advantage of his gifts and his time with us, we invited Professor McGowan to drop by the local Catholic high school, where there was a workshop in progress. The workshop involved students from the eight Catholic high schools in the board who were busy preparing for the end-of-October Pilgrimage, a walk to a holy place (Sunday Eucharist). In each school, the pilgrimage has as its theme struggling communities in the developing world and particular questions of justice. The Pilgrimage experience explores the need for awareness about and education on the theme, and provides the opportunity to respond in some small way through prayer and fundraising. The overall hope, of course, is for a sense of responsibility to develop and stick with staff and students, and concrete participation in opting for the poor. With the students, Professor McGowan reflected on the Beatitudes and how we are called to be people of the Beatitudes.

The evening presentation on the *Year of Faith and Catholic Social Teaching* was a clear invitation for each of us to live our baptismal priesthood as priest, prophet and king. This theme was summed up beautifully by the parishioner who thanked Mark McGowan for reminding us who we really are: we are defined by our Baptism. Increasingly, the culture wants to define us simply as taxpayers and consumers. October 3—a day that was well planned—became a day very rich in meaning and understanding of the gifts we have and of the challenges we face as parish community and as Catholic education community.

October 10

Thanksgiving Masses for the Three Elementary Schools

Here we are at Thanksgiving already! During the week before Thanksgiving, each Catholic school community makes its way to the church for the celebration of Eucharist. As I mentioned earlier, the local Catholic school board provides the bus transportation, which is very helpful. Another visit to the parish church is an opportunity to welcome the children (and some of the parents and grandparents) to *their* church. As most of the children are not present regularly at Sunday Mass, we emphasize that this is their parish and their church. Thanksgiving is also an invitation for us to connect the family celebrations of this holiday with the Eucharist as the ultimate expression of thanksgiving.

The children's participation comes easily, as we use Eucharistic Prayer II for Children, with sung responses throughout. The liturgy is introduced by one of the students who is charged with helping prepare the Mass. An important part of the introduction is the reference to the baskets of food collected by the school for our Food Bank. These baskets are carried in procession. Food drives in the schools are another concrete example of the social capital the parish has in the Catholic school community.

October 15

Blessing of ECKP Addition at St. Kevin School

I am off to visit the school that has built an addition to accommodate the Early Childhood Kindergarten Program. The addition consists of two large classrooms and an office. With the province of Ontario's introduction of all-day kindergarten, this addition was necessary. I believe that this change in approach is a positive one. Perhaps in an ideal world it would be better for children to stay home with mom or dad. But our culture is anything but ideal. Daycare is an enormous need these days. Generally, it is an economic necessity for both parents to work. The price for daycare is steep; daycare spots are too few. The day-long program is a relief for many families. When it comes to learning and reading, children from middle-class and upper middle-class families have an advantage, since much pre-school education happens at home. This is not usually the case for children from lower-income or lower-literacy families. Full-day kindergarten can be a plus for these children.

I think the same thing applies to faith learning. I believe strongly that many of the children in our schools are now being formed in their faith more at school than at home. I often think of that sentence from the Ontario Bishops' 1989 letter, "This Moment of Promise":

> Given the increasing fragility of families and the overextension of parishes, it is becoming more obvious that the school for some, is often the primary place where young people experience the Church as an alternative community

shaped more by faith, hope and love than by the values of a consumer culture.

That observation was written some 25 years ago. How much more true it is today. It is clear that what happens in those early years in the Catholic school plays a key role in helping to form a Catholic imagination.

October 20

Blessing and Distribution of New Testaments to Grade 4 Students

This Sunday, the Grade 4 children of the parish and their families have a special invitation to be present at Sunday Eucharist. Mind you, that invitation is there every Sunday, but since we are dealing with a pernicious culture that provides too many distractions, Sunday Eucharist is generally not a priority. Yet there is a more positive response to Sunday Mass when the children are somehow featured. That is the case with the Grade 3 children during the blessing and distribution of the rosaries. For the parish, this becomes an occasion for the families and children to renew their relationship with their parish church. The Sunday assembly, too, profits from the Grade 4 children being singled out and invited to come up and receive a copy of the New Testament. It is a visual statement for all present to look at and pray for the future church standing before them. Grade 4 is selected as the appropriate time, as it is in this grade that the students begin to study the New Testament.

After the homily, the priest celebrant prays, "Father, bless these bibles and grant that these children who use them may grow in wisdom and grace before you and all your people." The teacher then calls each child by name. The child comes forward and the priest says, "Receive from the Church the Good News of Jesus Christ." (He then touches each child on the forehead, lips and chest with the New Testament.) "May it touch your mind, your lips and your heart." The ritual takes but a few minutes. And because the blessing is directly focused on the Word of God, this becomes a rich moment in the homily to elaborate on the power of God's Word in the Bible and on scripture-based prayer. The New Testament touching the head, the lips and the heart of the child becomes a compelling gesture, reminding us all of how God's Word touches every aspect of our lives.

October 24

Rite of Commitment for Confirmation

The Sacramental Guideline for the diocese describes preparation for the sacrament in these words: "The purpose of the immediate sacramental preparation is to dispose the candidate to receive the grace of the sacrament and to participate fully in the liturgy of Confirmation." In bold print is added, "it is not intended to prepare candidates for a test of their religious knowledge." We find that the three ritual moments leading to Confirmation—The Rite of Acceptance, the Rite of Enrolment and the Rite of Commitment—are effective means of assisting young people preparing for the sacrament.

The Rite of Commitment is the third and final ritual for our Confirmation candidates in their journey towards the sacrament. Candidates are invited to bring with them their Baptism candles. Most are able to do so. We assemble in a quiet area of the school. Here again, this ritual would make a powerful statement if we did it in a Sunday assembly. But experience tells us that too few would be present. A 20-minute prayer experience at school becomes for the candidates a prayerful moment to see and experience the connection between their Baptism and Confirmation, which is a completion of Baptism. On behalf of the parish, the teacher presents the candidates who are completing their preparation for the sacrament. The priest then asks the candidates to focus on the Easter candle shining in their presence. Reference is made to their Baptism and the sponsor who lit their Baptism candles from the Easter candle. This time the candidates are invited to come forward themselves, in a symbolic action of owning their Baptism commitment, and light their Baptism candles from the Easter candle, praying that indeed they may work at becoming the light of Christ.

October 27

38th Annual Pilgrimage for the Poor in the Developing World – Notre Dame College School

This journal entry is particularly personal. As mentioned earlier, the Catholic high school in the parish we serve was started in 1947 by the English Canadian Holy Cross Fathers. My first assignment as a Holy Cross Father was to teach religion and French at the school. After a sabbatical in France to do further studies in adult catechesis, I returned to Notre Dame College School to teach religion. In 1976, I proposed to the principal and several key teachers at the school the idea of a pilgrimage—a holy walk. This idea had been percolating in my mind since my studies in Paris. During my time abroad, I participated in a pilgrimage, walking with university students to the magnificent cathedral of Chartres. I was very taken with pilgrimage as metaphor for faith and life. I envisaged three catechetical/pedagogical pillars that would serve as a foundation for a Catholic high school to commit to such a pilgrimage: fundraising to support projects in a developing country, witnessing to faith and educating for justice.

The fundraising effort of Miles for Millions, a Canadian campaign launched in 1967 to alleviate world hunger, had ended. This created the opening for a similar initiative. The idea of being sponsored for each kilometre walked was attractive, with the money raised going to support both a Holy Cross mission in Bangladesh, India or Peru and the Canadian Catholic Organization for Development and Peace. Fundraising is one pillar of the pilgrimage, but only one.

The pilgrimage is a walk to a holy place. The faith experience is the second pillar of the pilgrimage. As there are no shrines of note in our area, the holy place becomes the school gym. The pilgrims meet together on the morning of the last Sunday in October for prayer and commissioning, and then walk for 10 kilometres before returning to the school gym. On the walk, some carry wooden crosses and banners. At the destination, the school gym, we celebrate the Eucharist, the Mass for the Progress of Peoples. The Eucharist concludes with

a candlelight service of commitment to work at living out one's Baptism and be a voice for those in need.

The candlelight service has proved to be very rich for several generations of students. The gymnasium is darkened. Then one flame becomes visible as the Easter candle is carried into the gymnasium. Pilgrims and their families and friends listen to a commentary on the candle and flame, linking it to the light of Christ received at Baptism. Little by little, from the one candle, the light spreads throughout the assembly. The liturgy ends with a community commitment to continue the pilgrimage, each in his or her own way. The faith dimension, putting feet on the gospel, is a second pillar shaping the pilgrimage experience.

The preparation for the walk that takes place in the school and across the curriculum for some three weeks before Pilgrimage Sunday is the third pillar to the pilgrimage experience. This is education for justice. Each year, for over 38 years, a different question of justice and peace has been presented. The question has become an opening to reflect on Catholic social teaching. In the early years, a world broken by unshared bread was the organizing theme. Pope Paul VI's *On the Development of Peoples* served as a lens through which to study such a broken world. In the 1980s, it was Pope John Paul II's encyclical letter *On Social Concern*. We look at contemporary social, political and economic realities from several perspectives: the preferential option for the poor, solidarity, the common good, the integrity of creation, interdependence, the primacy of persons over things, and other elements of Catholic social teaching. This year, the focus is the relationship of our consumer habits with the sweatshops in Bangladesh. Educating for justice is a vital piece of the pilgrimage experience. The educational objective is to furnish the students with a critical sense, so that they do not simply accept what they see or read. We want to alert the students to the reality that in our culture operates a dominant ideology whose values and choices are often in opposition to the values of the gospel. And we want to encourage the students and awaken within them the ideal that we live in an interdependent world, that we are all responsible for one another. This approach flies in the face of the individualism and general indifference to caring for the common good that unfortunately are becoming the hallmarks of our contemporary culture.

After 38 years, the pilgrimage has stood the test of time. This indicates that there is something good here, something important in the life of a Catholic high school. There is no way such an experience would survive and even thrive without in-school imaginative leadership and an exceptional staff committed to the ideals of the pilgrimage. From Notre Dame College School, other Catholic high schools have borrowed the pilgrimage idea, adapting it to their own local reality. At Notre Dame, the pilgrimage has become a point of reference for how a Catholic high school can live its Catholic school difference. Certainly, having the pilgrimage in the early part of the school year (October) is a great help with the bonding or community building that one wants for every Catholic school community. And over these 38 years, more than $2 million (counting some matching funds from the federal government) has been raised for development projects and disaster relief in the developing world.

NOVEMBER 18–22

The Confirmation Experience

This is the week we celebrate the sacrament of Confirmation at the parish. This year, as usual, there are more than 100 candidates for the reception of the sacrament. The church can accommodate at most 650 people. That means we must have three different Confirmation liturgies—one liturgy for each of the three schools in our boundaries. The day before the liturgy, candidates come to the church for the sacrament of Reconciliation and for the rehearsal. This is another instance of the cooperative spirit of both the school board and the school leadership, providing the time out of school and busing the students to and from the church. Confessions take place after some solid moments of preparation. Candidates listen to and reflect on the Word of God, with the aid of some pertinent questions meant to help the candidates get inside their hearts and come to know themselves more honestly. The quality of the confession experience deepens when the classroom teacher can spend some time beforehand talking about the meaning of the sacrament: what sin is and how helpful and even therapeutically healthy the Reconciliation experience can be. While much of the content of the confession tends to be routine, there are those few instances when the penitent reveals a remarkable understanding of who she is, or what he feels sin is doing to his outlook and approach to life, and how he really does desire to change. After the sacrament of Reconciliation, and with the help of the teachers, the candidates walk through the procession and responses that they will need the next evening during the celebration of Confirmation.

On the evening of Confirmation, candidates and sponsors meet in the parish hall to prepare for the procession into the church. Our local bishop, Bishop Gerard, is outgoing and friendly; he likes to visit with candidates and sponsors beforehand. He sees Confirmation as a privileged time for pastoral visits to parishes and as a time to connect with young people and their families. Before the Mass begins, we explain to the assembly that there will be a collection during the liturgy, with the funds directed to our service of the poor.

The theology of Confirmation is perplexing; the age for Confirmation is questionable. It is clear that Confirmation is a sacrament of initiation. Confirmation following Baptism serves to prepare and initiate the person into the Eucharist. It is this theology that is proposed in Vatican II in the *Constitution on the Sacred Liturgy*. In 2007, in his exhortation *Sacramentum Caritatis,* Pope Benedict XVI writes:

> It must never be forgotten that our reception of Baptism and Confirmation is ordered to the Eucharist. Accordingly, our pastoral practice should reflect a more unitary understanding of Christian initiation.

The order of the sacraments is clear: Baptism followed by Confirmation to initiate the person into the Eucharist. This is the order in the restored Rite of Christian Initiation for Adults. Generally, this order obtains for adults. With children, the age question and the order question surface. In a few dioceses, the practice has changed to reflect preparation for the Eucharist. If First Communion is in Grade 2 or 3, Confirmation takes place before then. In most parts of the Canadian Catholic world, it seems to be the practice to receive Confirmation in Grade 7 or 8, well after one has received First Communion. The theology of a sacrament of initiation is operative, but more emphasis is given to Confirmation as entry into Christian maturity or the moment to say "yes" to one's Baptism.

While I prefer to see the sacrament in its proper place, between Baptism and Eucharist, I do understand why some bishops, or indeed many bishops, are reluctant to change. There is age-old meaning in the rite-of-passage idea, with Confirmation equipping one to live an adult faith. My experience over the years tells me as well that it is not a bad idea for Grade 8 students to have a bit of a time-out and to do some sharing, serving and praying in preparation for receiving the sacrament. The bottom line for me is this: Confirmation is a sacrament of the Holy Spirit. One receives the Holy Spirit. This is beautifully expressed in the Confirmation liturgy. So if one is confirmed at Baptism, one receives the Holy Spirit; if one is confirmed in the RCIA moment of the Easter Vigil, one receives the Holy Spirit; if one is confirmed in Grade 2, one receives the Holy Spirit; and if one is confirmed in Grade 8, one receives the Holy Spirit. *Veni Sancte Spiritus!* Come, Holy Spirit!

November 26

An Unusual Entry into the Journal – A Christian Anthropology

In an earlier phase of my ministry as a Holy Cross Father, I was a religion teacher at our local Catholic high school. As a religion teacher, I believed that a faith that would sustain the students should be presented so that they could apply it in a practical way to how they look at life and how they live life. I saw the social sciences as a means and help in educating in the faith. So I developed a course on vocation, marriage and the family that borrowed from the sociology of the family and a social analysis of our culture, and I created a course on the social teaching of the church using economics and politics, especially the politics that promoted peace.

All of this background is an introduction to Marco, a memorable student who, like more than a few of my former students, is now teaching in the local Catholic school board. Marco is at the technology end of things. He works out of the board office. He is a high-energy guy with an unbelievably creative imagination. Marco has groups of students doing business and entrepreneurial studies. But he is always concerned about the faith and ethical dimensions of the content of education. He thought that I would be just the person to offer a reflection on faith and business to some 75 students participating in a business and entrepreneur workshop at the Catholic Education Centre. I thought about it and put together what I termed "The Challenge of Christian Anthropology."

I began by observing that, for the most part, society defines a person as a taxpayer and a consumer. For politicians we are taxpayers; business people see us as consumers. The spiritual dimension, or what has to do with the soul, has been privatized. But I insisted that the soul and the things of the soul are central to who we are. (I added that the difference between public education and a Catholic education is that the Catholic school must be concerned with educating—with tending to and taking care of the things of the soul. If we are not doing that, we should throw in the towel.)

I then asked the students to fast forward X number of years and to imagine: "You are on your deathbed … you try to come to grips with your mortality … and with the question of eternal life. You are a Christian. You have tried to live as a Christian, a follower of Jesus, a believer in the resurrection. Does being a taxpayer really matter? Does being a consumer really matter? But does your 'spiritual life' … the life of your soul matter? Absolutely." All of this sounds much like a homily, but the question is profoundly important. As Christians, the things of the soul must be very much in control of how we live.

As we had just celebrated the Feast of Christ the King, I proposed a review of how we approach life from the perspective of Christ, the Lord of history and the Lord of all creation. The following questions helped me shape what a Christian anthropology might look like:

- What does Christ the King want?
- How would Christ the King order things?
- Where is Christ's rule on earth?
- How do I live out the kingship of Jesus in which I was baptized?

Then I suggested that these questions should be applied to the very real problems and situations one encounters in the business world, the so-called real world:

- Look at our environment, at the natural world, at the ecology question. For example, consider the ongoing devastation to earth, wind and water caused by extracting oil from the oil sands. How would Christ the King want us to relate to the physical world?
- Look at the relationships between nations and peoples. Is there any situation where Christ the King would take the decision to go to war?
- Look at the world's energy supply and food resources. What would be the mindset of Christ the King: to hoard and gouge, or to share and see that no peoples go without the essentials for a life with dignity?
- Look at our use of power—globalized corporate power—Bay Street and the Toronto Stock Exchange. Would not Christ the King operate on the principle that the needs of the poor have priority over the desires of the rich?
- Look at the world of culture and entertainment. Christ the King would have questions for us about time and money spent—or wasted—on the quality of "the stuff" we engage in. Do our culture and entertainment build up people and society, or do they demean, dehumanize, tear down and exploit?

- Look at the way indigenous peoples, our First Nations peoples, are treated—especially in northern Ontario, in our own province. Would the political strategies and approaches we have implemented so far be accepted by Christ the King?
- Look at the homeless and refugees. How would they fit in Christ's Kingdom?
- Look at the unborn, those with serious physical limitations, the very old, and people with dementia. What place would they have in Christ's Kingdom?
- Look at how our government runs. How would political strategies and decisions be made in the office of Christ the King?
- Look at my own choices and decisions and priorities. Look at yours. Christ is the King of the entire universe, including your and my own personal domain. What would he think of the way we live our lives?

I wanted to take this opportunity with the students to challenge today's dominant ideologies. A person is much, much more than the politician's taxpayer and the marketer's consumer. Responding to these questions invites the students to move beyond the taxpayer/consumer categories; it challenges them to see people and structures as Christ the King sees them. This is a whole new way of looking at the person. It is a Christian view of the person and of the nature of his or her relationships.

November 25

News of *Evangelii Gaudium*— Pope Francis' *The Joy of the Gospel*

Today we received news that Pope Francis has issued an apostolic exhortation on *The Joy of the Gospel.* It is interesting that the news comes first through the secular media. I learned of it through the CBC website, followed by reporting in *The Globe and Mail* and *The Toronto Star*. It is exciting to see how Pope Francis seems to have captured the imagination and attention of so many, and that a document on the mission of the church would receive such attention. Of course, the secular media would mine this exhortation to try to find changes in church doctrine regarding abortion, homosexuality and women priests. They are quick to note that nothing changes. But then they do highlight some of Pope Francis' concern regarding the globalization of the economy and his critique of the trickle-down theory of economics. And for sure they lead with his passionate defense of the poor and the idea that our church must be a church of the poor and for the poor. A day or two later, my online church sites provide me with a more thorough study of the exhortation. I make a note to myself that since *The Joy of the Gospel* focuses on the church and preaching the gospel as a missionary endeavour, it deserves some serious study, especially given that we find ourselves increasingly in mission territory with the Catholic education project.

Pope Francis says this about mission:

> This is certainly what mission means. Consequently, an evangelizer must never look like someone who has just come back from a funeral! Let us recover and deepen our enthusiasm, that "delightful and comforting joy of evangelizing, even when it is in tears that we must sow …. And may the world of our time, which is searching, sometimes with anguish, sometimes with hope, be enabled to receive the good news not from evangelizers who are dejected, discouraged, impatient or anxious, but from ministers of the Gospel whose lives glow with fervor, who have first received the joy of Christ." (*The Joy of the Gospel*, 10)

November 25, 26, 27

Second Meeting with Parents of Children Celebrating Their First Communion at Easter

I am always a bit apprehensive on the evening the parents are to gather for some faith formation around the sacrament of the Eucharist. We "form" the parents so that they can be the primary educators of their children. Yet we do have those silent questions: How many will show up? What will the mood be? How many, though they show up, will resist, giving the impression that they would rather be anywhere else in the world than here? For these three evenings, however, our fears are allayed. There is a good turnout. Most people are on time. We start at 6:30 p.m. and finish just before 8:00.

Our session begins in the foyer of the church. We want to give the parents a sense of parish community; we want them to know that they are an important part of the parish community of St. Kevin. We describe the geography of the parish, pointing out that Catholics, no matter where they live, are part of a parish. The strategy here is simple: more than a few of these parents are here simply because their children attend a Catholic school in our parish. Outside of that fact, they have no real sense of membership in the parish. We want to invite them into owning their membership in the parish. We stress that, for us, registration in the parish is very important. We have about 3,500 families, and having people register helps us keep track of our members.

We also make a pitch for financial support for the parish. This would be under the rubric of "support of the church." (Full disclosure: In the nine years I have been pastor of the parish, I have never spoken about money for the upkeep or maintenance of the parish. However, several times a year, I do invite our community to support the poor, whether it be through Share Lent or our own social needs of food bank, soup kitchen or St. Vincent de Paul.) On this night for parents, I would omit this plea for financial support altogether, except the reality is that our seniors are dying. And the envelope users, the steady supporters of the parish, are the seniors. Financial support of the church is just not part of the culture of the occasional or secular Catholic. So we make this gentle plea. The idea is that we want the parents to be aware of our ongoing material needs as a parish.

Back to the foyer and our conversation with the parents. The purpose is to show how intimately linked Baptism and Eucharist are. We describe how the liturgy of Baptism unfolds. We share that here in the foyer, we welcome the persons to be baptized; these are usually infants, along with their parents and godparents. Many of the parents remember bringing their children here for Baptism. Then we invite the parents and friends to walk with the infant through the entranceway to the baptismal font. Over the entranceway or threshold of the church, there are icons of the twelve apostles. We point out that ours is an apostolic faith. It is the faith of the apostles, who experienced both the historical Jesus and the risen Jesus. This faith experience has been shared with us and we, in turn, share with our children.

We arrive at the baptismal font. The purpose of standing at the font is to show the clear connection between Baptism and Eucharist. Baptism and Confirmation initiate us into celebrating and receiving Eucharist. It helps us visually that the baptismal font has as its neighbour the twelfth station of the cross. Jesus is depicted dying on the cross, with the spear hole visible in his side. We are reminded of St. John's observation that from the hole in Christ's side flowed water and blood, the water of Baptism and the blood of the Eucharist.

We then walk the parents through the church, explaining the placement and meaning of altar and ambo (lectern), presider's chair, tabernacle, stations of the cross, Mary's altar, and reconciliation room. As well, we list different devotions and rituals (Rosary; blessing of throats; Ash Wednesday; celebrating saints such as Kevin, the patron of the parish; etc.) that mark us as Catholics. Then we take a few minutes to review with them the parents' book, *We Share in the Eucharist* (Novalis, 2009). This serves as an opportunity for us to encourage the parents to keep at it and to take seriously their teaching and guiding role with their own children. Two parents then share with the other parents their own very practical experience in preparing their children for First Communion. Finally, we walk the parents through Eucharistic Prayer II for Children, commenting on the words and the actions at the altar.

The response from the parents is generally positive. As they are leaving, many comment on how worthwhile the session was. Yet, in our own review, we feel that something was missing. There was very little conversation and sharing among the parents. We were too keen on providing them with different input and resources. We did most of the talking. That is not a great adult-learning model; it is something for us to work on.

November 29

Delivering Advent Resources for the Grade 4s

Every Advent, the parish provides resources, readings and devotions for adults, families and children in the parish to enrich their journey through the four weeks of the Advent season. These are left on a table in the foyer so people can help themselves. And each Advent we select one grade in particular and furnish teachers and students with Advent booklets to help them absorb the meaning of Advent as preparation to live again Christ's first coming at Christmas and to prepare for Christ's second coming.

December 2–6

Advent Reconciliation for Grades 4 to 7

For the students in the three elementary schools in the parish, we offer the sacrament of Reconciliation twice a year—in Advent and in Lent. Reconciliation takes place in the church. This is another instance of the local school board's generosity and commitment to the Catholic dimension of our schools, as they provide the bus service needed to transport the children from the schools to the church. We are also fortunate to have our confreres (Holy Cross Fathers) from our Community Centre down the street to assist us. We know how lucky we are. Most parishes do not have this luxury of good, available clergy. Usually, three priests assist us. Today, with 130 Grade 4 students present, we definitely need several priests. We have the students here for about 90 minutes.

Reconciliation begins with a welcome and an invitation to prayer. The large screen at the front of the church allows us to put text and prayer in such a way that the students can easily participate. The Word of God is followed by a brief reflection and application to their young lives. The Prayer of Sorrow leads into several questions for reflection, suggesting areas where love has given way to selfishness in their lives. Looking at their relationships with family, friends and God becomes the moment for them to own their own sins. Personal confessions follow. The common penance is a prayer or prayers projected on the screen. The students have brought with them reading material to occupy themselves before or after Confession. The teachers are present, but with the prayer and the reading, there is wall-to-wall silence in the church.

The Encounter in Confession

The preparation emphasizes Confession as a moment to renew one's friendship with Jesus. It is Jesus who invites; it is Jesus who listens; it is Jesus who forgives; it is Jesus who sends the young person on her way. The encounter in Confession is privileged time. It is clear from the conversation with the young person that he knows sin. The young person knows what it is to refuse to love when he opts for self over other.

It is interesting to chart the development of the young person from Grade 4 to grades 7 and 8. There seems to be more awareness of the sin reality in the older student. A minority of the older students show real maturity; self-awareness has developed. Some are perplexed as to why they do what they do and why their attitudes can sometimes control them, even when they don't like it. Some would rather be softer and more loving in their relationships with parents and siblings and friends. Among these young persons, prayer has become important—prayer that is personalized, rather than just a saying of prayers. That, I find, is a real grace of the sacrament of Reconciliation: to be able to listen and talk to and encourage the young person in his or her spiritual journey. The interplay of grace and friendship with Jesus and prayer and sin solidifies the Catholic imagination. Ultimately, it is not about being mean to brothers and sisters and disrespecting parents, or the little lies and deceits committed along the way. It is about experiencing Jesus and his mercy and deepening their friendship with Jesus.

December 8–9

Rite of Inscription for First Communion Children

This weekend is Inscription Sunday. At three of the Masses, the Grade 2 students who are preparing for First Communion at Easter are present with their families. The parish will formally welcome them and then encourage them on their way. We are very pleased with the great turnout of children and families. Of more than 100 candidates, only a half dozen or so are absent. These we will contact in the days to come. After the homily, we ask this question of the students: "Children, do you want to say yes to the invitation of Jesus to come to his table and share his life with him?" Together the children respond, "We do!" And we ask the parents: "Do you ask the Church that your child receive Jesus Christ in Holy Communion … and do you promise to continue to help your child prepare to receive Jesus as the bread of Life?" And the parents answer, "We do!" Finally, we ask the assembly: "Do you, the people of St. Kevin's parish, promise to support these parents and children by your prayer and the example of your living faith?" And the assembly exclaims, "We do!"

Each child then comes to the altar to receive a certificate. On it is inscribed these words:

> The Parish Community welcomes you to the table. You are a special child of God. You belong to God's own family. On Sunday, you gather with the family and you listen to stories of God's love. Now you are preparing to receive Jesus in your First Holy Communion. You will share this day with your family and with the church family. We are very happy for you.

This ritual takes only five minutes or so. It is especially rich for the children, as it sharpens their anticipation, allowing them to come to the altar now in preparation for the first time they will receive Jesus in the Eucharist. And for more than a few of the parents, for whom Sunday Eucharist is not a regular part of their weekly routine, this is a time to refresh their experience of Sunday Eucharist, gather in prayer with the assembly of believers, be called by the Word of

God, and come to the Eucharistic table prepared for them. This is the experience we want them to share with their children. Finally, for the parish community, the event highlights the sacramental dimension of parish life and the urgency of praying always. Pope Francis has said, "Jesus leaves us the Eucharist as the Church's daily remembrance of and deeper sharing in the event of his Passover. The joy of evangelizing always arises from grateful remembrance: it is a grace which we always need to implore." (*The Joy of the Gospel*, 13)

December 9–11

Sacrament of Reconciliation for the Catholic High School

It is time to head off down the street to the high school for the Advent sacrament of Reconciliation. There are eight parishes around the high school. Our parish is the largest.

The school is always working on ways to make the Reconciliation experience rich for the students. Long experience tells me that if there is a classroom conversation of some quality touching on the meaning of sin and of the peace and healing that come though the sacrament, there is likely to be a positive response from students coming to Reconciliation.

I don't want to be negative here, but it seems that not many teachers do much preparation in the classroom before the students head off to the auditorium for a brief prayer service and examination of conscience before the sacrament. Furthermore, I think that makes sense. The saying goes that you can't get blood out of a turnip! You can't give what you don't have! My gut tells me that not many of the teachers seek out this sacrament themselves. So they are not likely to sincerely encourage the sacrament for others. I think I can say the same for most people in the parish. These days, very few seem to avail themselves of the sacrament of Reconciliation. Why this is so, I don't know. Is it because we have collectively lost a sense of sin? Maybe there is a little of that. And maybe there is a sense that deep sorrow in one's personal prayer is sufficient for forgiveness from a kind and merciful God.

Many folks miss the days of a communal penitential liturgy with common absolution. I am among their number. I can recall absolutely packed churches during Advent and Lent for some beautiful and deeply meaningful liturgies. But then the rules changed. Often I say to myself—what a loss! Now it is only one-on-one personal Reconciliation. As a confessor, I know well the power of one-on-one confession. I have experienced great healing and peace in receiving the sacrament; also, I have been privileged to preside at this sacrament and relate with people who have experienced that same peace and healing. I am sorry that so few take advantage of it. I do feel that it is very important that we continue to offer these one-on-one sacramental moments for students in our Catholic schools.

As I observed for the younger children, this can be an opportunity to encourage the young person to pray, to offer some brief spiritual direction. It is also a time for some personal reckoning, a time to realize that one is a sinner and that one is always in need of God's loving mercy and forgiveness. The high school chaplaincy leader does a very solid job in preparing the students for the sacramental encounter. On this occasion, it is the religion classes that are being invited to the sacrament. All come to the prayer of preparation, but not all will come to the sacrament. That is up to each individual. Usually, three or four priests are available for the sacrament.

December 12

Annual Faith Formation and Luncheon for Priests, Trustees, Principals, Vice-Principals and Managers (10:45–1:30 p.m.)

The local Catholic school board works hard at fostering the relationship between the schools and the parishes. Today is the day for the annual luncheon for priests and parish pastoral workers, principals and chaplaincy leaders of the schools, along with trustees and administrators. Usually, the bishop of the diocese addresses the gathering. Today, Bishop Gerard spends some time highlighting Pope Francis' *The Joy of the Gospel.* As well, he very generously offers a copy of the exhortation to each person present. The meal, an

Italian *pranzo*, is always delicious. The fellowship of priest with the principal or principals from his parish at table together allows for a different and more relaxed conversation. Yet, "How worthwhile is this get-together?" is the cynical question I ask myself while driving home from these encounters. For example, how many of the participants followed what the bishop was saying or are going to spend any time at all studying *The Joy of the Gospel*? Eventually, in my musing, a more positive reflex surfaces. Many of the clergy are from elsewhere and are not accustomed to the Catholic school reality here in Ontario. It is healthy for them to see the equality of relationship and collaborative partnership that can exist between priest and principal. The priest does not dominate or control what goes on in the school. It is good for the clergy to see that there is a unified Catholic school board/diocesan team in operation. And it is very important for the principals to see how supportive and encouraging the bishop is, and how the clergy appreciate the work of the principals. There is much wisdom in the idea that table fellowship can succeed in ways that formal meetings can't.

December 16–18

Advent-Christmas Masses for the Schools

In the last week before the Christmas holidays, the schools come to the parish church for the Advent-Christmas liturgy. These are exciting days for the children, especially for the little ones. It is fun to watch them parade into the foyer of the church, bundled up in their winter outfits. I marvel at the teachers of the early years who are responsible for getting the kids ready to go outdoors in cold weather. Teacher, thy name is patience! As usual, the children who will process with gifts and artifacts that help to introduce the liturgy or who will proclaim the Word are well prepared. But this year, unlike in past years, we experience a wee bit of uneasiness. By "we," I mean the pastoral staff, and by "wee," I mean very, very little!

We have structured this school Mass in our *Green Binder* guideline to reflect Advent and get into Christmas. This year, though,

Advent seems to have been forgotten. It is all Christmas. Thus our uneasiness. Reflecting on the situation, it seems that, with our emphasis on Advent, we wanted liturgical purity. But the hearts of the kids, and probably their teachers as well, were very much into Christmas. With a number of parents and grandparents present, this was a moment for the school and the children to sing the carols and tell the story and mime the Bethlehem scene. In a way, this really is popular religion, doing Christmas as a Catholic school community a week before Christmas; when we look back at it, that is probably the way it should have been. Likely next year we will try for just a little bit of Advent, at the beginning, maybe—*O come, O come, Emmanuel!*

December 16

Planning Meeting with Principals and Pastoral Staff

The last week before the break is the time to meet with the principals of the four schools in the parish and with the chaplain of the high school. We welcome them to the rectory for lunch and for the planning meeting. We have prepared a draft outline of the parish-school activities from January until the end of June. The principals come with their calendars. It is important for us to know the dates for EQAO testing. We must stay clear of those days. This scheduling is so much easier than it was in the days before the *Green Binder*. Once the draft becomes final, we will prepare refills for the *Green Binders* at the schools. That way the principals have no surprises. Even when changes do arise, this doesn't seem to pose a problem, as we have established a good working relationship between the schools and the parish. From our point of view, the schools are always very accommodating.

The meeting is also a time for the principals to connect. For the pastoral staff, it is a learning experience to be privy to what is happening in the schools with staff, with parents and with the board. We become more sympathetic when we hear what these women and men are dealing with. The planning is followed by lunch, some great sandwiches from the local Italian delicatessen, and a small glass of Prosecco—to toast our partnership and salute the holidays.

JANUARY–JUNE

January Reality Check
Parish Ministry

Back in August, I seized on the idea of this journal to record the points of relationship and cooperation between the parish and the Catholic schools in the parish. As a Catholic educator, I have always been convinced that the Catholic school is a very rich *locus pastoralis*, or pastoral area for evangelization. As the years have gone by and the secularization process has become more aggressive, I am convinced that the church must go to where the people are. Up to a few years ago, it was the people who would come to the parish … to the church. It is clear now that, in most cases, this is just not happening. Yet here in Ontario, we are very blessed with a fully funded Catholic school system. Some may be upset that kids and their parents do not come to church, but the reality is that they are Catholic. And the new reality is that the church must go to them. That is my understanding of the new evangelization! I have always believed that we can do that effectively through Catholic education. So I am keeping this journal to document the many ways a parish can do that pastoral outreach to the schools and, more personally, to review what may need to change or what can be added to enhance our ministry to the schools.

At the same time, I do not want to give the impression that Catholic education and the Catholic school are the only parish ministries we do. With 3,500 families in the parish, we have a number of active committees: Liturgy, Pastoral Council, Stewardship, Social Justice. We have an active RCIA program, youth ministry program and Catholic Women's League. That Man Is You, the men's program, meets every Saturday. We have funerals—too many funerals—and Baptisms: as many Baptisms as funerals. We have pastoral visits and sacramental ministry in seniors' homes and Holy Communion visits for the homebound. We have Baptism- and marriage-preparation programs. In a word, our parish experience is like most other parish experiences.

Our ministry in our Catholic schools is a parish priority. It is possible largely because we plan for it, structuring it into the overall ministry of the parish. Such planning done collegially with the schools makes for some effective and joyful evangelizing.

An Update

I noted in the introduction to this journal that we are two Holy Cross Fathers ministering here at St. Kevin's. I have been pastor for the past nine years. My confrere, Father Vijay, has been here for four years. Father Vijay is a member of our Indian Holy Cross community. He did his theological formation at Regis College in Toronto, and is now ministering with us in Canada. Our animation of the parish is very collegial. On January 1, we switched roles. I took on the associate's role and Father Vijay became pastor. The workload pretty well remains the same for both of us—heavy!

JANUARY 9–14

Two-Hour Sessions with Specialist High Skills Major Students

Responding again to Marco! Marco is the coordinator for Student Success at the board office. Each time I say yes to Marco, I am never quite sure what I am getting myself into. At the high school level, there is a program called the Specialist High Skills Major. The way I understand it, this is an umbrella program over and above the courses the students take. Students are summoned together at certain times for input on different themes. Generally, the students are specializing in business and accounting courses or a construction program and even some arts courses. The themes presented give them a more well-rounded understanding, stretching somewhat the borders of their discipline. The invitation is for me to spend a couple of hours with the Specialist High Skills Major group from each high school, concentrating on three areas: personality inventory, conflict resolution and ethics.

In a sense, these sessions are a deviation from the regular pastoral animation we exercise in our Catholic schools. While we are often asked to visit a class and answer "church" questions, or to present church teaching on different subjects, this invite is a little outside the usual box. I agreed to do it because I thought I would learn something about where the students are at, and I might be able to impress upon them how interesting and how important or relevant social ethics are for high school seniors. In the back of my mind, I also thought it would be good for the students to encounter a priest working on these questions in the classroom.

The agenda was to visit four high schools, which turned out to be three because of a snowstorm. Each group consisted of about 20 students. I have been out of the classroom for close to 20 years—I must admit to having more than a little apprehension and even fear: Would I be able to connect? I prepared as best I could. For the personality component, I used the Myers-Briggs Type Indicator test available on the Internet. The students seemed to take to this. Most claimed that their particular letters (representing *Introvert / Extrovert*; *Intuitive / Sensing*; *Thinker / Feeler*; *Perceiver / Judger)* fit them. I was able to apply the interpretation of this test to whatever they might be doing and how they might be relating with people now and in the future.

I then used a scheme for conflict resolution based on win–lose negotiating (International Conflict Resolution) or win–win negotiating (Domestic Conflict Resolution). Years ago I used this model from Conrad Grebel College, University of Waterloo, in a Peace Studies class. I was surprised at how apt it still is for everyday living. For the students, this approach applies to family and friends. But the exciting part of the session for me was to engage the students in different applications of Catholic social teaching. They showed some interest, and on various questions, there was a definite option the students would make for the poor and the oppressed, for those suffering injustice. They really got the hang of interdependence: how it can be negative and how it can be positive. The Development and Peace campaign *Are you listening? An ombudsman will!* puts in relief both negative interdependence (the devastation several Canadian mines are inflicting on countries in the developing South, with community displacement, water pollution and soil erosion) and positive interdependence (the Canadian church's response to local churches in the developing world that have asked Canadian Catholics to intercede with our members of Parliament on their behalf and on behalf of the poor to appoint an ombudsman who will listen to their complaints and act for justice).

I was intrigued to find out the source of students' information about what goes on in the world. In the past, the trick was to coax the students into thinking critically. In these sessions, it struck me that the same trick is needed today. Though I was unable to spend a lot of time on this topic, Catholic social teaching implies a certain grasp of the social situation. What are the sources of students' understanding of context and question and social problems or, to use the jargon of the day, *how do they interface with the world*? I am sure that social media play a big part in shaping their knowledge. But that in turn makes me wonder about accuracy and credibility. When I was teaching, I would always challenge students on sources: What is the credibility of this source? What biases does this source have? Whose interest informs the news from this network or this newspaper? I still believe that, for social media or for traditional media, these are the critical questions in dealing with social ethics.

January 16

Green Binder Inserts and Delivery

Over the last few days, we have been preparing updated versions of our school contacts for the January–June term. The structure remains the same. Dates for meetings change; in some cases, selections of readings for Mass and formulations of letters to be sent home to families also change. We visit the schools to deliver the inserts for the binder. This is also a time to do some planning around a Grade 6 project deriving from the current Development and Peace education project.

January 21

The Phone Call

The phone call today contributes to the colours and contours of contemporary Catholic education. The man on the line was a parent whose children attend a Catholic school on the other side of the city. He is a Catholic. His three children, none of them baptized, are in the Catholic school on the strength of his baptismal certificate. He now wants the children to be baptized. He is calling us on this side of the city because he is having trouble with his own parish priest. The priest will baptize the two youngest children, but the oldest child must meet the parish priest for catechizing and preparation for Baptism. The gentleman on the phone is balking at that. His idea is that the boy should be baptized along with his younger brother and sister. I commented that the priest's request was not unusual. We would do the same here. After some conversation back and forth, I suggested that the priest might allow a teacher to prepare the boy for Baptism. The dad countered that the priest said he would do it himself because he had no faith in the religious education at the school.

This set the parent's problem in a new light for me. I asked him why it was so important for him to have the children baptized now. He said that his grandmother, now deceased, had stressed that the children must be baptized, and he was pursuing this out of fidelity to her. He was very emotional on this point. I then asked him about his own faith, wondering if he might prepare his son for Baptism. There was an abrupt "No!" He did not go to Mass. He did not know much about religion. Baptism was simply the water and the words. And with the water and words, he felt that he would be all right by his grandmother.

I gently insisted that the gift and privilege of Baptism make demands on us. We profess ourselves as Christian; we commit ourselves to living in a certain way described in the gospels as light and salt for the earth; we prepare to receive Jesus in the Eucharist; we accept the cross that comes with following Jesus. The man on the phone was just not buying this. His Sundays were his own. All he wanted was the water and the words for his children. As the conversation progressed, I was thinking that this was a case of the cheapest of cheap grace. I wrapped up the conversation, asking him to rethink the priest's request. It would be good for him to sit in on the conversation his son would have with the priest. The phone call terminated amicably.

Over the next few days, I found myself thinking about this exchange. The father represents a number of parents who see Baptism as a passport to entry into the Catholic school. I have met any number of such parents. Usually, however, I do detect a certain openness and goodwill on the part of these parents, and a certain guilt at having put off Baptism for so long. I can't read hearts, but I do sense that there is faith there, at least some faith. I am not sure about my telephone partner. It is not mine to judge. But he wants membership without any participation or ownership. That runs counter to our evangelization. His attitude tells me that there is little hope that his children will be brought up in the Catholic Church. I am equally disturbed by the attitude of the other parish priest. I know that not all of the teachers in our Catholic schools have the ideals and commitment we would like them to have. But to completely dismiss the faith education that takes place in the Catholic school smacks of clericalism at its worst. I believe that in our contemporary Catholic education project we find both the parent of cheap grace and the cleric on the pedestal unable to minister, with laity living out their baptismal priesthood as Catholic educators. Not a happy combination to have to deal with in an ongoing way!

January 23

It's Back!

Here is the headline from today's *Globe and Mail* op-ed page: "Chapter and verse, Catholic school funding's unfair." This threat to the existence of our publicly funded Catholic schools is never out of sight for long. This time it is columnist Konrad Yakabuski, a regular in *The Globe*. I find myself in disagreement with most of his positions. Perhaps it is a slow news day today, and he has had to go back into his file and bring out one of his whipping stones. Today it is Catholic education. As it happens, I was mulling over the Catholic education survival question during the Christmas break. I have been developing a reflection on pretty much the same content covered by Yakabuski's article and on other voices singing the same anti–Catholic education song. I believe that, to safeguard our future, it is critically important for those of us in the Catholic education community to understand our arguments and to reinforce our own position and the logical coherence of our position. Ultimately, I believe that this is best accomplished by doing Catholic education with as much grace and generosity as possible, faithful to our mission and continuing to answer the call of our vocation. I entitle my reflection "The Shifting Sands of Publicly Funded Catholic Education, or Navigating the Slippery Secular Slope! Surviving in an Uncertain Social and Political Climate." (It is found in Part Two—Pastoral Theological Reflection.)

January 29

Mass for the High School Staff

Today is transition day at the high school: the end of the first semester and preparation for the second semester. The chaplaincy leader at the high school, always alert to possibilities for faith nourishment for the staff, arranged an optional early morning Mass. Father Vijay, the pastoral minister for the high school, is very pleased: about 50 teachers were present, showing great attention and participation. The gospel about the sower of the seed and the different types of soil for the reception of the Word of God is very apt for teachers. Father Vijay made the point that we are present this morning at Eucharist because someone helped us, assisted us in sowing God's Word among us and for us. Someone assisted us, preparing us, tilling the soil so we could receive God's Word. Now we recognize again our own vocation as Catholic teachers, to assist the Lord in helping our students prepare to receive God's Word, deepening their own faith.

January 29

Catholic Schools and Parish Harvest Kitchen Meals

I have mentioned how the relationship between the parish and the Catholic school becomes mutual gift. In our own way as a parish, I think we add much to the school community and the education offered at the school. It is a plus that the school is attached to a parish community. We are a support and a help to the school as it works to live out its mission as a Catholic school. For us here at the parish, as well as being the source for our evangelization outreach and a contact point for sacramental ministry, the school is social capital, providing us with volunteers and leadership. We can do things that we would not even think of doing were it not for the participation of teachers from our schools. (It helps that more than a few of the teachers are also members of the parish. It's one of the benefits of living in a small city.)

The Niagara region of Canada has suffered a great deal due to the closing of plants and factories. Unemployment is high. Judging by the number of food banks and soup kitchens across the region, poverty is very real. From November to the end of April, every Wednesday afternoon/evening we offer a hot meal in the parish hall.

Tina and Anne, two of the teachers from the high school, are the coordinators for what we call our Harvest Kitchen. (The program started as Out of the Cold, but about ten years ago, a few churches and civic groups got together to fund a hostel that welcomes guests overnight.) Cooking teams from the parish alternate with the culinary arts department of the high school in preparing the meals for 85 to 90 guests. And along with parishioners, students are present to chat or play cards with the guests before supper, serve the meal, and clean up afterwards. The participation of the students often begins as a way of getting their mandatory service hours done, but many students continue to serve simply because it is a good thing to do.

The Harvest Kitchen experience is genuinely owned by each of the four schools. The three elementary schools take a Wednesday, and with support from staff and parents, the students provide the evening meal. It is always more than just a meal, though! Often the school choir performs, and students make placemats and center centre-pieces for the tables. The high school is the mainstay, with the chef of the culinary arts department taking the lead in preparing meals at least twice a month. The coaches of the basketball teams bring their players at least once every Harvest Kitchen season to do the serving and cleaning up. While the senior students act cool about the whole thing, conversations later reveal that for many of them, the experience has touched their minds and hearts. The experience of Harvest Kitchen becomes a very rich and practical "religion class" for the schools, for both students and teachers. They encounter some in the community who, for different reasons, have a difficult time being totally independent. They have needs. There is service. This is what we are invited to do by our Baptism and by being a friend of Jesus. There is also witness. Seeing the adults who organize and prepare allows the students to understand that this is the church and this is what the church is called to do. It is a concrete example of Catholic social teaching. Pope Francis expresses this:

> An evangelizing community gets involved by word and deed in people's daily lives; it bridges distances, it is willing to abase itself if necessary, and it embraces human life, touching the

suffering flesh of Christ in the other. Evangelizers thus take on the "smell of sheep" and the sheep are willing to hear their voice. (*The Joy of the Gospel*, 24)

February

Right about now it starts. Parents begin calling the office for the Baptism certificate of their little one as they look to register the child in kindergarten at the local Catholic school. Part of the new culture of Catholic education is that Baptism is the passport that gets the child into the Catholic school. Unfortunately, it is Baptism, the certificate, more than Baptism, the sacramental reality in the little person's life that is the ticket. For more than a few parents, this is the first connection with the parish since the Baptism of their child three or four years earlier. Yet it is something. Our Catholic schools are good schools. For any number of reasons, parents want their children in our schools. I really do believe that one of those reasons is a concern about the faith development of their child.

February 3

Feast of St. Blaise / Blessing of Throats

The reports from the schools are positive. Principals have organized the blessing of throats for the classes in their schools. The prayer service is important; it signals that it is not just a gimmick or random event when someone turns up in a classroom with a pair of candles to say a prayer for protection of people's throats.

In the introduction, St. Blaise is identified as a bishop and a martyr. The story is told of how he healed a little boy who was choking. The need to pray for good health is emphasized. Jesus' words in St. Mark's gospel about healing the sick are proclaimed. There is a brief intercessory prayer for family members, for the sick and for healthcare workers. Each student comes forward, and the principal or teacher places the crossed (unlit!) candles against each student's throat, under their chin, to ask God's protection for the health of the person.

Even as a young boy, I felt there was something special going on when the candles would rub against my neck. Touch and the use of the candles make this devotion something more than just a prayer. The candles add an element of mystery for the child. Because of the candles, he or she will remember this sacramental or prayer. The experience is one of many that helps to develop a Catholic imagination. This morning's 8:00 Mass offered concrete evidence of the impact of St. Blaise on the Catholic imagination; instead of the usual 50 or 60 people, over 150 attended. Folks were coming for the blessing of throats at the end of Mass.

FEBRUARY 4

High School Gay-Straight Alliance

This afternoon was special. It's not something you will find in the *Green Binder*, as the invitation came out of the blue. A few weeks ago, Stephanie, the chaplaincy leader at the high school, invited me to drop in to an after-school meeting of the Gay-Straight Alliance (GSA) club. For me and for the high school, this structured approach to being supportive of gay youth and to those questioning their sexual orientation is new. Recent provincial legislation dictates that every high school must provide such a club or group if there is a request for it. This is the second year of the GSA club. The year before, a few students put together a proposal for the club. Along with the chaplaincy leader, they went to see the principal, and thus this group was formalized. This afternoon there were six students. I was introduced and welcomed warmly. The club has more members, both gay and straight, but six came to this afternoon's meeting.

According to Stephanie, this is a safe place for these students. At the beginning, she established a set of ground rules. Because Notre Dame is a Catholic high school, the GSA club must be sensitive to the school's Catholic reality, just as the school is sensitive to the students' gay reality. That means no promoting same-sex marriage at club meetings. Regarding intimacy, Catholic teaching holds that sexual intimacy belongs only in marriage, so at the GSA club, the students do not have conversations of an erotic nature.

The students seem okay with the ground rules. They are pleased to be able to meet. The time together is very informal. There were two points of business at this encounter: to prepare for the February 26 Pink Shirt Day, which happens in the middle of multicultural week, and to continue to discuss how the school's GSA club might make a presentation to the staff regarding the students' concerns. Pink Shirt Day is an opportunity to address directly the homophobia—either explicit or implicit—that exists in the school. The students are preparing Pink Shirt Day posters, which will be placed throughout the school. The question of the presentation to the staff is more involved. It is a work in progress. The conversation among the students revealed that some teachers are very sensitive to the LGBTQ (Lesbian, Gay, Bisexual, Transgendered and, for the school, the Q means Questioning) reality. These teachers are quick to call attention to bullying language or behaviour. Other teachers can be tone deaf to such bullying, either on purpose or through an ignorance that is not very benign.

Further conversation with Stephanie provided an insight into the fragility of some of the students in the GSA club. Such students must live with the consequences of bullying: fear, low self-confidence, bouts of depression, constant anxiety and personal confusion. For other students who are gay but have not come forward, it can be even more difficult. Stephanie is very good. She is cool. She knows that the existence of the GSA could be a landmine. But she is extremely supportive of the students who meet with her once a week.

Homosexuality is never an easy question in the church. That goes for the Catholic school as well. Indeed, our culture continues to be marked by heavy strains of homophobia. Stephanie finds some healthy grounding and direction in the American bishops' 1997 pastoral message, "Always Our Children: A Pastoral Message to Parents of Homosexual Children and Suggestions for Pastoral Ministers." I gave Stephanie a copy of "LGBT Ministry and Catholic Social Teaching," which I came across only yesterday (*Ministry and Liturgy*, February 2014). The article highlights key themes of Catholic social teaching—human dignity, common good and justice—that can be a foundation for LGBT ministry. I left the meeting grateful for having been present and aware that journeying with these students with such sensitivity adds an important dimension to Catholic education, a dimension I had never really considered before.

February 5

Meet with Grade 6 Teachers on Development and Peace Ombudsman Project

Today is the follow-up from the brief mid-January meeting with the Grade 6 teachers on the Development and Peace ombudsman project. The teachers came by the parish after school. They had gone through the material for the project. One member of the parish Social Justice Committee, a Grade 6 teacher in a school outside the parish, had worked out a guideline showing how the project fit perfectly into both social studies and religion expectations. The teachers were very excited and enthusiastic. Matt exclaimed that his students really get into questions and experiences that have to do with social justice. This is religion teaching made easy. For me, this was gratifying to hear. This project was not intended to be a burden on the teachers—something extra they had to do.

They were equipped with the student activity guide and the theological backgrounder focusing on principles of Catholic social teaching: the sacredness of creation, solidarity, the option for the poor, the common good and integral human development. Gary, from our Social Justice Committee, also attended the meeting; he will serve as a liaison with the parish. The target date for completion is the end of February. In the foyer of the church this weekend, just a few days before Ash Wednesday, we will assemble the projects from each Grade 6 class. The display will serve as a reminder of Share Lent and the invitation to do both charity and justice.

February 6

Grade 8 Journey Retreat

The local Catholic school board provides for an overnight Grade 8 retreat for each elementary school. The retreat takes place in a school that has been repurposed as a spiritual centre. The renovation works well. The theme for the retreat this year is *Journey,* based on the Emmaus story from St. Luke's gospel. The two-day experience is put together in a way that challenges the students to open their eyes to recognize God's presence in their lives and in the world. There are community-building exercises, a nature walk, journalling times, an introduction to prayer, meditation time and eco-justice activities. The elementary chaplaincy leaders for the board provide oversight for the retreat. The Grade 8 teachers and two high school students join the permanent retreat team in animating the retreat. The parish comes into play on the second day, when we celebrate Eucharist with the students and their parents, who are invited for the concluding evening Mass and supper. The *Journey* team does a very good job communicating the retreat program and suggested Mass texts with the parish. Today is the third and final *Journey* retreat for our parish.

The retreat is a rich experience for the students. This is faith formation that takes place in a non-classroom environment. Over the years, Grade 8 teachers have remarked that the retreat can be an excellent bonding experience for the class. The parish priest is welcome to spend lots of time with the students during the retreat in addition to the Mass, but, because of the time factor, this is difficult to do. Presiding at the Mass also means spending some time with parents. It is good to have a moment to pray with them and to pray for them and their children. The trick here is to be positive and encouraging. The moments of Mass and supper become clear examples of the reality of the triad—home, school and parish. I never miss the opportunity to point this out and to celebrate this unique feature of a Catholic education.

For the students, I always refer to the Easter candle, situated in the chapel room close to the altar. The candle is a tangible sign to which I can attach all that Baptism means: becoming a disciple of Jesus, wearing a Baptism robe of Christian values and instincts and ways to act, being a light in whatever situation we find ourselves, realizing that we have been anointed and called especially by the Lord.

Certainly the program is charged, and from all reports, the agenda is substantial and works very well with the students. I give credit to the teachers and those called to monitor the students through the night hours. But something is missing in this experience. Our sense here in the parish is that the liturgy, the celebration of the Eucharist, needs more attention. For an hour, we have a privileged community of students and parents. But too often, students and parents are passive. There is little or no response to the invitations to pray or to lift up our hearts. The music accompanying the celebration is hit-and-miss. Often, the music fails to engage the assembly.

The parish must accept some of the responsibility for the uneven liturgical celebration. Our assumption has been that the team and teachers are on top of readying the children for the Eucharist. But it is clear that they need our participation and direction. For the animation team, more is needed in terms of liturgical formation and imagination in celebrating with students and parents. A deeper understanding of liturgy is called for. As for the parish, we need to collaborate with the Grade 8 teachers and students well before the retreat. This critique can also be directed at the board and at the diocese to provide liturgical formation and resources for the animation team and for the teachers. I am sure that we are not the only parish that has this experience. An hour of Eucharistic liturgy with parents and students is such a rich opportunity, but such an hour must be planned carefully, with an understanding of how powerful the liturgical experience can be. I believe this critique applies not only to this particular experience, but to most of our prayer time with students in our Catholic schools. Generally, at the level of parish and diocese and board and school, we have a lot of liturgical formation work to do with our teachers.

February 10

Visit to Prayer Corners in Schools

During a conversation after Sunday Mass, Liana, a Grade 3 teacher, mentioned the prayer table in her classroom. That really piqued my interest. Today I took a little time and visited the schools, popped into classrooms to say hello and had a look at prayer tables or prayer corners. What a revealing experience. A principal claimed that every classroom is expected to have such a table or corner. Would that this were the case! My sense is that prayer tables are more common in the early years and junior grades. The Bible, the Word of God, is enthroned on the prayer table. Maybe "enthroned" is stretching it somewhat, but the open Bible is central to the prayer tables I viewed on my visit. A crucifix hangs above the table. A rosary or a class set of rosaries is included on the table, as are bible storybooks, stories of the lives of the saints, and a box of prayer intentions. Several teachers use tablecloths that are in sync with the colours of the liturgical year. In a few classes, the prayer service that is used once a week is placed on the table. Candles, plants and even painted stones or small rocks are visible as well, all with a certain meaning attached, shared by the students and their teacher.

Two thoughts of a pastoral, theological nature struck me in reflecting on my prayer table visit. In the everyday classroom experience, the prayer table is evidence of efforts to integrate faith with the curriculum. It is not simply that the table and devotional aids are present on the table; in chatting with the teachers, I understand that this corner of the classroom is more than cosmetic. Prayer happens. References to the crucifix are made. Attention for classroom prayer is directed at the prayer table. Prayer intentions are placed into the jar or box. While the teacher may be the architect of the prayer table, in most cases, the students are the builders. And while there are set times for referring to the table, this happens at other times, too—the timeout times from whatever they may be studying, because a teachable faith moment arises. A second thought has to do with the power of the Catholic imagination. Especially in the early years, children need something concrete to help them connect with the Lord: a crucifix, a statue, a rosary, a candle. The contents of the prayer table can support the children as they develop their faith imagination, their Catholic imagination. This is especially important for so many of the children who experience very little formation into the faith at home.

February 19

Meet Grade 3 Parents—
Formation for the Sacrament of Reconciliation

The Pastoral Guideline for Sacramental Preparation for Children in our diocese states that "all children who are to receive First Eucharist are to be prepared and have the opportunity to celebrate the sacrament of Reconciliation prior to First Communion." We are faithful to this guideline in our First Communion preparations. In the classroom, the teachers begin to explore with the students the idea of sin and the meaning of reconciliation. The priests then visit the classroom and chat with the students about Confession. At the Grade 2 retreat, each child comes to the priest with a sin or two, asks forgiveness and receives absolution. We have entrusted the sacred duty of formation for Eucharist to the parents, where it naturally belongs. The parents of our Grade 2 children concentrate on formation for the Eucharist.

Pastorally speaking, we feel that a more rigorous formation for Reconciliation is in order. We reserve that formation for Grade 3. We charge the parents again to be the primary formators of their children. Early in February, we send home a letter with the Grade 3 children from all three schools in our boundaries, inviting the parents to come to the church for a formation evening. With the letter, we include as a resource a booklet entitled *Your Child's First Penance*, by Carol Luebering (St. Anthony Messenger Press, 2000); this booklet outlines the challenge for the parent in preparing their child for the sacrament of Reconciliation. This brings us to the formation and information meeting this evening. We welcome the parents and invite them into the church. The response is not bad: about 60 to 70 percent of the parents have responded.

We begin by describing our parish experience with the sacrament of Reconciliation and the children in our Catholic schools. Here we share the outline of the Reconciliation services we offer in Advent and Lent; we also point out the physical places in the church where the priests are stationed for Confession. We add here how

Confession changes through the years as a young person changes, journeying from being the child of Grade 4 to a more mature teen of Grade 12. More than a few of these young people develop a real openness and seriousness towards the sacrament.

A second moment is to move from the children to the parents present with us. If one is to form the child, the adult must have a grasp of the power and the beauty of the sacrament. We describe the need to forgive and to ask for forgiveness. We stress the importance of a pause, a spiritual time-out in our lives to identify the drift and to reboot a gospel perspective on life. We consider the reality of sin. We point out moments in the gospels when Jesus forgives and makes whole again. We present the three main players in the sacrament: the person, the priest and Jesus, who is the most important player.

We then present to the parents the resource *We Prepare for Reconciliation* (Novalis, 2009), a companion text to the First Communion resource we use with the Grade 2 students, *We Share in the Eucharist.* This excellent resource moves from reflecting on the God who gives life, love and joy to the God who gives peace and forgiveness. The dynamic of the book is very similar to the Grade 2 resource and therefore is familiar to the parents. The teaching mandate is also the same. The Grade 3 teachers have class sets of this resource, and will help prepare the children in class. However, the primary teaching role, we stress, remains with the parents at home. In concluding, we invite the parents to bring the children and themselves to the formal reconciliation liturgy that will take place towards the end of May.

February 25 to 27

Third Formation Meeting for Parents of First Communion Children

This week we hold the third and final session with the parents of Grade 2 children who are preparing for First Eucharist. This date was set strategically just before Lent. In the tradition, we know that Lent is the time for intense preparation for Baptism and the other two sacraments of initiation: Confirmation and Eucharist. We want to encourage parents to seize the moment and provide the necessary formation for their children. The participation was not bad. We are looking at hosting another such evening to accommodate the 12 parents from the three schools who, for various reasons, could not be present. Such absences are not surprising. Unexpected things always come up; for example, the kids are sick or parents' work hours have been changed. And probably a very few hold the attitude that they have something more important to do, and so a church meeting can wait.

Aware of our concern from the last session regarding how passive the parents were, we proposed a change in format. In the letter to the parents reminding them of the meeting, we included three questions for them to reflect on beforehand:

- What questions is your child asking?
- What is working for you as the First Communion teacher?
- What are you learning about yourself in this process?

We devoted the first 30 minutes of the 90-minute session to sharing in groups of two and three on these questions. We then took ten minutes for reporting or gathering some feedback. Given that most of the parents did not know each other, this was not an easy exercise for them. For parents to disclose what they shared was like pulling teeth. Yet they did offer some rich responses. They liked *We Share in the Eucharist* very much—the prayers, the pictures, the opportunity to write in the book, the stories. The questions the children posed included "What does the host taste like?" "How will I know when to come forward?" "How is this host Jesus?" "Why do I have to wait until Easter Sunday to come to Communion?" During the parents' conversation time, I chatted with the Grade 2 teachers. Here my question was simple: "Do you think the parents are doing much at home?" Generally, "yes" is the answer, qualified by "some more than others." For the teachers, it is very clear in class. Some students will note that they have already done this section or that part of the book. From the talk with the teachers, my sense is that this is the minority of the students. So from this part of the session, I arrive at three conclusions:

- Even if the parents are lax or inconsistent, it is good that they are charged with this teaching role, as they are the first teachers of their children. This emphasizes the great importance that the parish and the Catholic school give to faith and to the sacramental life of both children and adults.
- It is good as well that we have the backup of the classroom teacher, who can supply the formation that some children may be missing at home.
- And the three sessions of the entire formation experience for the parents are very worthwhile as adult faith formation and as privileged moments for the parents as they connect with the parish and come to the church. This provides a concrete reminder that they are members of our parish.

From the conversation segment of the evening, we moved to a review of the sacraments of initiation. We did this by describing the RCIA experience in the parish, highlighting the Easter Vigil, which leads to the new Catholic Christian coming to the Lord's table for the Eucharist. We wanted to show that Easter makes great good sense as the day for First Holy Communion. Then the parent member of our team gave a brief exhortation, coaxing and challenging the parents to use Lent as a privileged time for praying with the children and preparing them for Easter Sunday and First Communion with the family. The parents on our team (Angela, Kelly and Nadia) distributed a Lenten calendar they had prepared for the group, suggesting faith activities and sections of *We Share in the Eucharist* to take up on different days of Lent. The team member also gave to each parent a copy of another resource to help them with their children's questions: *25 Questions About the Mass* (Novalis, 2010).

We then mapped out how the five Easter Sunday Masses would unfold for First Communion. Each child would be signed in at a special table so that the celebrant would be able to share the names of the children with the assembly after Communion. (The table is in the foyer of the church, and on this day balloons float above the table so it is easy to find.)

Explaining how the class's First Communion would take place a few weeks after Easter Sunday was the final item on the agenda. We were very sincere in our thanks to the parents, and issued them a modest certificate from the parish acknowledging their role as First Communion teacher for their child. The hope and prayer of our parish team is that maybe—after the emphasis and the encouragement and the resources distributed and the example of other parents given—maybe the Lenten season will provide the environment for some parents who have not done much yet to seize the moment.

February 28— Weekend before Lent Begins

I made a quick trip to the schools today to share some Lenten resources the parish had ordered for some classes. Each year we select a booklet of Lenten devotions for children for a particular grade in the schools. This year it is Grade 5. I delivered a class set of *These Stones Will Shout Out* for the Grade 5s at each of the three schools. The prayer booklet is a help to the teacher and becomes a daily reminder to the student of the meaning of the 40-day Lenten journey. For the Grade 7s, we have two resources from Development and Peace. First, a study guide entitled *There is food enough for everyone and yet nearly one billion people around the world are suffering from hunger.* It is based on the Share Lent theme inspired by Pope Francis—*One Human Family, Food for All.* Second, we offer them a well-crafted Share Lent calendar created by a parish in British Columbia. The calendar highlights the issue of world hunger and proposes small but important gestures a person can do to participate in feeding the hungry and giving drink to the thirsty. We also give this resource to the Grade 8s.

We are happy that there is always two-way traffic between the schools and the parish. The schools today also make a quick trip to the parish, as the Grade 6 teachers bring the displays their classes have created for the ombudsman social justice project. Members of the parish Social Justice Committee drop by, and we install the project in a corner of the foyer. The artwork and collage of written letters to members of Parliament make it clear that the students understand well the damage to human communities and the devastation to the environment that result from irresponsible and selfish mining practices. Their project is a visual reminder that our faith must be a faith that does justice, and that religion is found in all aspects of life.

March 5

Ash Wednesday Mass at Schools

Lent has finally arrived. We have a morning and an evening Mass in the parish. It is always encouraging to welcome folks to Ash Wednesday Eucharist. For each Mass, the church is just about full. I take this as a signal that all that Lent means—sacrifice and renewal and the journey towards Good Friday and Easter Sunday—is still very much alive in the hearts of people.

And through the day we celebrate Ash Wednesday with the Catholic schools. In the morning, Father Vijay goes to the high school for two Masses and the imposition of ashes for the staff and students. I celebrate Mass in two of the elementary schools, while one of our confreres from Holy Cross Centre House celebrates Mass in the third school. Ash Wednesday is the one day of the school year that we have Mass in the elementary schools. On all other occasions, the students come to the church. The *Green Binder* contains an outline for what we need to celebrate Mass in the school gym: a table to serve as the altar, a white tablecloth, two candles, a lectern, four small dishes for the ashes, larger bowls of water, and a towel. The schools already have the readings they need to prepare. I bring the missal, ashes, altar bread and wine, chalice, corporal, purificator, four ciboria vessels for Holy Communion and, of course, my vestments.

It is a joy to celebrate Ash Wednesday Mass in the school gym. There is an intimacy with the students that we don't have in the church. In spatial terms we are close. The kids are sitting in rows on the floor. I sit in my chair. I emphasize that it is the Catholic

School community that embarks on this Lenten journey, and that Lent is both personal and social. The readings are taken from the children's lectionary and are geared to their understanding. I find myself interrupting the Joel reading to explain why all of the people must come together to fast and to do penance. And with the reading from St. Paul's Letter to the Romans, I can stop to give some colour and contour on what it means to be an ambassador for Christ. This way, the reading really does become a practical faith story for the children. The moment when they come forward to receive the ashes is important for them. Again, this is an element of laying the foundation for the Catholic imagination. Somehow we are close to God, and God is present to us in ritual and in symbols. I don't give a long homily, simply a brief word explaining what we are doing and why.

However, I do emphasize living Lent through some type of sacrifice. I share with the students my approach to Lent since early childhood—"What are you giving up (or doing) for Lent?" That was the question my parents put to me. That ought to be the perennial Lenten question, the challenge somehow to connect with Jesus' suffering and sacrifice for us.

MARCH 10–14

School Break

MARCH 18

A Reconciliation Service at School for Grades 4 and 5

Advent and Lent are the two seasons when we offer the sacrament of Reconciliation in the schools. Given that Lent comes fairly soon after Advent, we do things a little differently in Lent. For the children in grades 4 and 5, we go to the schools for a penitential service. While we are fortunate to have the priests of our religious community close by, it is not always easy to line up confessors. And yet, we do want the students to experience Lent as a penitential season, to have the chance to peek into their own hearts and consider how they are doing in loving their family and friends and reflect on how their friendship with Jesus is going. We have given the school a PowerPoint program of our prayer service. We count on the teachers to do some preparation with them around the themes of forgiveness and being sorry for their sins. The students assemble in the gym. We listen to the Word of God (the Parable of the Lost Sheep), which assures us of God's love for us no matter what and calls us to repent and turn back to the Lord. We reflect on some probing questions intended to help the students review their own relationships and their friendship with Jesus and with others, and together we pray, asking the Lord to forgive us and restore us to his friendship.

There is a moment for a brief instruction urging the children to remember that it is Lent and encouraging them to do something for Jesus, who carried his cross for all of us. In all, we spend about 30 minutes at each school. It's an important moment that reinforces for the students that our God is a God who forgives and always wants us to enjoy his friendship. As well, it becomes a moment to further emphasize the meaning of Lent as a season for each Christian to personally identify with the suffering Christ. The time and the experience add colour and detail to the young person's Catholic imagination.

MARCH 18

Catholic Education Alliance Committee

Back in 2010, I was invited to serve on the local Catholic Education Alliance Committee. The purpose of the committee was to share ideas and activate strategies at the local level on how we may defend and promote Catholic education. Members of the committee came from the various Catholic education partners—trustees, teachers, principals, parents, elementary and secondary students, parish priests and unions. I was the parish priest representative. For close to two years, the committee was quite active. Goals were established and contacts were made. Then the committee became dormant for about 17 months. Now a new committee is in place. Happily, many new members are joining, and a few of the original members remain.

I am one of the survivors. The fact that the bishop, board chair and director of education serve as co-chairs underlines the importance the Catholic school board is giving to the work of the committee. It is a worthwhile effort to bring together different voices and perspectives to reflect on the vision and practice of Catholic education.

Today we are having a luncheon meeting. The first part of the meeting reviews earlier activities and recommendations. This is followed by an open discussion on the gift of Catholic education and what it means. All agree that, with our Catholic schools, we have something special. More than a few claimed that the Catholic school is *just different*. It seems that this is something we know intuitively! There is an almost evangelical fervour in the room. It is good to experience the young people and adults sharing from their own perspectives and talking together with such passion. The refurbished committee will meet frequently. The challenge will be how to move from good feelings about a Catholic education and the workings of a Catholic school to a clear demonstration that the social fabric in Ontario would be diminished without Catholic schools. How to make folks aware that Catholic education really does contribute to the life of Ontario?

March 19–20

Sacrament of Reconciliation: Grades 6, 7 and 8

The senior elementary students come to the church for the sacrament of Reconciliation. Grade 6 students arrive in the morning, Grade 7s in the afternoon, and Grade 8s the next morning: about 130 students per session. As usual, they have brought some reading materials with them to occupy themselves while others go to Confession. Teachers organize students' entry into the church. They file in, dipping their fingers in the holy water and making the sign of the cross, and demonstrating a variety of attempts at genuflection before going into their pew. The purple banners in the sanctuary remind the students that this is a Lenten experience, as does the welcome question on the big screen, which asks, *What are you doing for Lent?* The service, on PowerPoint screens, guides the prayer. Several of the prayers are prayed in common. We comment on one brief prayer emphasizing the involvement of each person of the Trinity in the life of the student:

> Father, you created me and put me on earth for a purpose. Jesus, you died for me and you called me to complete your work. Holy Spirit, you help me to carry out the work for which I was created and called.

This is a powerful little prayer, because it invites the students to see that their vocation and purpose in life is to work at accomplishing the project that God sets aside for them. And really, this has to be one of the fundamental reasons for Catholic education—to assist young people in discerning God's call in their lives. If we believe that because of Baptism we share a common priesthood, then a Catholic education must help young people to understand what it is to live out their baptismal vocation.

One of the screens is entitled *Some hard questions to consider.* This serves as an examination of conscience. The rapidly changing culture, which shapes the young person, becomes more of a challenge for us as priests and faith animators. Young people live the culture, but in many respects, we are strangers to much of what they live. The teachers are closer and more connected. A teacher frames the question for us: "Do you engage in cyber-bullying, saying mean things without having to face the person, through texting, email, Facebook, etc.? Do you post mean or embarrassing pictures / things online? Do you choose to look at inappropriate pictures / videos on the Internet?" These days I often find myself asking some of the teachers, "What should I know? Where are the kids at?" Even the vocabulary stumps me at times. A very articulate Grade 6 girl with uncommon insight into her own soul and the movement of the Holy Spirit in her life shared how argumentative she is and how quick she is to lose it. She exclaimed that something happened, and she went "supernova"! Not understanding the vocabulary, I could guess that she became quite angry. (A *supernova* is the explosion of a massive star lighting up the constellation.) A teacher later explained how "supernova" is used by the kids—an eruption caused by frustration and anger.

A recent conversation with a priest from a neighbouring parish led to an exchange about the value of what he called "assembly line" confessions, where all the kids come to Confession one after the other. In a way, I can appreciate his point. How valid is the experience when there is so little freedom? And yet, I do believe that having elementary students come to Confession in Advent and Lent is important because it allows them to

- experience the forgiveness that comes with encountering Christ in the sacrament
- spend time in the parish church during one of the great penitential seasons of the church
- have one-on-one pastoral care through a two- to four-minute conversation with the priest, which can be a type of spiritual direction
- receive affirmation, encouragement and, at times, a gentle challenge to follow Jesus more closely and make Jesus a part of their life
- create a memory that may well be activated sometime in the distant future: that the sacrament of Reconciliation is always available if they experience a crisis in life and are looking for understanding and healing.

March 25–26

Sacrament of Reconciliation at the High School

If last week was more assembly-line confessions with the elementary students, this week, with the high school students, is more freedom of choice. This semester, the religion classes come for the time of preparation, prayer and reflection. Then the students are invited to participate in the sacrament. Priests are available during four periods a day for the two days. While they did not come in the numbers we experienced in Advent, students did come to

Confession. After a while, I am struck by how hard some kids have it in life. Does the hurt and complication of life come with the stress of being a teenager? Does it come from peer pressure or fear or a dysfunctional home life? Wherever it comes from, it seems to cause depression in some students. Many students also experience academic stress and worry about their post-secondary choices. The confession conversation allows them to unburden themselves a bit. The priest has the opportunity to listen and to console and to encourage and to pray with the student. The confession experience itself reveals an important slice of adolescent reality. And it provides a little insight into the adolescent spiritual/religious life. Young people do believe in God, and they do pray … sometimes. But generally, church and regular Sunday religious practice are not high on their priority list.

I am working on this journal entry on Wednesday of the third week of Lent. The first reading at Eucharist today is from Deuteronomy. From year to year, in reflecting on this reading, I stay with the words "But take care and watch yourselves closely, so as neither to forget the things that your eyes have seen nor to let them slip from your mind all the days of your life; make them known to your children and your children's children" (Deut. 4:8-9). For me, this passage captures the core of the mission of the church—to remember, to not let our faith realities slip from our mind, to share them with our children and our children's children. Breaking down the mission of the church to the parish and to the Catholic school, I appreciate more and more the importance of the religious and liturgical life the students experience at the Catholic high school. While it is messy at times, not as neat and categorical as some would have it, in the Catholic high school we find *the remembering and the making known*! There is nourishment and guidance for students' baptismal faith. There is a forum for the important questions students have concerning faith and the meaning and purpose of life. There is an adult believing community that offers direction and encouragement to students, so that their faith may be a faith that does justice. As a church, how fortunate we are to have the intentional Christian community of the Catholic high school to help us in the remembering and in the making known!

MARCH 31

The Rite of Christian Initiation for Children

Since September, when the invitation was issued to parents who would like their children to receive First Communion here in the parish at Easter, we have been working with a group of ten Grade 2 children whose parents, or at least one parent, are baptized but who themselves are not baptized. (Question: Why have these children not yet been baptized? Answer: Any number of reasons, but one common reason seems to be "We just didn't get around to it," which can be interpreted as "It was not important for us at the time.") The children are in the Catholic school on the force of a parent's Baptism. Now that their children cannot celebrate First Communion at Easter unless they are baptized, Baptism is important! We accept this as it is and believe that somehow the Holy Spirit is present in all of this.

These parents have asked that their children be enrolled in our RCIC (Rite of Christian Initiation for Children) program. During these ten one-hour sessions, half of them taking place in the fall and the other half in Lent, a parish catechist has been meeting with the children, leading them to an understanding of Baptism and First Communion. Now, only one meeting remains before Easter. The parents of the RCIC children have participated in the three First Communion formation sessions for parents. The RCIC children will be baptized and then receive First Communion with their families at a special Easter Sunday afternoon Eucharist. We are blessed to have an excellent, very experienced catechist doing this formation work with the children.

APRIL 1

Retreat for First Communion Children

Most of the Grade 2 students will celebrate their First Communion at an Easter Sunday Mass in the company of their families. In the weeks following, the children will have a special First Communion Mass with their classmates. As I have mentioned, the

ideal we present to the parents at the beginning of the Grade 2 year is that they are the first faith educators of their children. We have met with the parents to form them and furnish them with resources to prepare their children for First Eucharist. As well, the Grade 2 teachers have worked at preparing the children for First Eucharist.

The final formative moment for the children is a half-day retreat in the parish hall, animated by members of our youth ministry team, with the assistance of the teachers. There are about 35 students from each school. Three schools means three retreat mornings. The youth ministers use all sorts of techniques in calling forth the children's imagination to come to know and understand God's goodness. For example, pretzels become praying hands; Cheerios depict God's circle of life, without beginning or end; Skittles represent the variety of shapes and colours and uniqueness of people in the world; Fritos convey the importance of salt and the gifts God gives to each person to make each one special; and marshmallows become the softness representing our emotions and feelings and persons with special needs, such as the elderly and the sick. The youth ministers make great use of various exercises and crafts to lead the children into appreciating the Eucharist as meal and sacrifice. At a certain moment, our pastor, Father Vijay, talks to the children about mercy and forgiveness. Then there is time for each child to come to Reconciliation. (Although the more formal preparation for Reconciliation takes place in Grade 3, students celebrate this sacrament at the retreat in Grade 2.) The reflective observer marvels at this retreat experience, and wonders why all faith formation, no matter what the age level, cannot be as engaging and as effective as the Grade 2 First Communion retreat!

April 13—Palm Sunday

THINKfast

For several years now, the high school chaplaincy team has collaborated with members of the parish Social Justice Committee to hold a THINKfast every Palm Sunday. Development and Peace has excellent resources to give purpose and insight to such an experience. I have become part of the program, spending about 30 minutes mid-day reflecting with the students on "thinking" and "fasting." For the thinking input, I stress how important the social teaching of the church is and how it must be applied to what is happening now in the common life we share. That means surfacing some political, economic and social situations that we must critique.

Why do many government policies seem to favour those with money, and why does the lower-income 20 percent of the population seem to fall further and further behind? How come the government is so ready to lend an ear to the energy sector and yet so deaf to treaty rights and concerns of First Nations people and so blind to the fragility of the environment? I then present some thoughts on fasting and on the religious tradition of fasting going back to Old Testament times. Fasting today is an important spiritual discipline in the great religions of the world. In our Christian experience, one fasts for several different reasons: as an act of forgiveness of sin; as preparation to take on a particular responsibility or ministry; as creating time and space to make a decision; as a means for uniting oneself with the Lord, emptying space so that the Lord may enter more fully into one's life; as a means of going without so that others might benefit. I point out that this is what the students are doing: fasting and raising some money to share with the poor. The day ends with the students participating in the 5:00 p.m. Palm Sunday Eucharist at the parish. About 75 students are doing the THINKfast this year. Together they walk up to the church from the high school. Students have prepared for different roles in order to participate in the Mass. Three of them are readers for the proclamation of the Passion. Others serve as ushers. After the Eucharist, the students eat soup and fresh bread in the hall. The experience itself is the most important part of this exercise. It helps, too, that this little group will add about $2,000 to the Share Lent collection.

APRIL 16

Grade 7s—Stations of the Cross

It is Wednesday of Holy Week. This is one of my favourite faith-education experiences of the year. Today we welcome the Grade 7s, who come to the church for the telling of the story of the last 24 hours of Jesus' historical life. We have an hour-long session for each school. Essentially, this is the stations of the cross, but we do it in story form. We receive the students in the foyer. We encourage them to dip their fingers in the holy water font and to bless themselves as they come into the church. The holy water calls to mind their Baptism, which means their discipleship. Holy Week makes great demands on their discipleship. Working with a group of 30 or 40 students and telling the story of the Last Supper, the Passion and the crucifixion is very rewarding. Because of the time, Holy Week, the power of the story itself, and even the secular reverence shown Good Friday and Easter Sunday, the students, by their focus and attention, show that they know this is important. And then there are the stations themselves, the images depicted on the stations, which add a video effect.

At first, the group gathers before the altar. We begin the story with the Last Supper. The connection is easily made between the table of the Last Supper for the Passover celebration and the Eucharistic table, the altar and the Lamb of God, and what we do at Mass. The emphasis is also on foot washing and what that means for the contemporary disciple.

It is then a simple matter for the students to turn to their left, where, at a glance, they can take in the first four stations of the cross. Now it is a case of expanding on the gospel accounts of the Passion. (There is more than a little intensity on the part of the priest doing the storytelling, because our sense is that likely most of these kids would not have experienced the Palm Sunday Passion liturgy or will not experience the Good Friday liturgy. And these gospel accounts are so rich for our faith.) I tend to dwell on certain stations that have great meaning for me: Jesus judged and condemned; Jesus meets his mother, Mary; Jesus and the women of Jerusalem; and the death of Jesus, with Mary and the beloved disciple at the foot of the cross.

At the conclusion of the Passion story, we pray before our Lenten Crucifix of the Crucified Christ, a prayer station we provide in the church through Lent. It is a metre-high crucifix from Cusco, Peru, the work of the indigenous Peruvian artist Edilberto Merida. The crucifix is done in the *ceramica grotesca* style, depicting the suffering and pain experienced by the campesino farmers in the high Andes. The Christ here replicates how these Christians depict the death of Jesus. We stand before the crucified Christ and we pray to the Lord of Mercy, the Lamb of God who takes away the sins of the world, for forgiveness for the sins of the world. Among the sins in our litany are these: the billions spent on weapons of war while millions starve or go without clean water and basic health care; the aborted infants in our area and across Canada; the tendency to demonize the poor for their plight in life; the children across the world enslaved in the sex trade; the peoples of the First Nations in Canada, many of them living in inhuman conditions; the insistence on tax cuts over social spending that builds up the common good. We conclude by asking, "Lord Jesus, continuing to suffer today in the suffering of your people, have mercy on us!"

Some Holy Week Reality Therapy

More than 15 years ago, I worked on a committee for the Institute of Catholic Education (ICE), which produced *Ontario Catholic School Graduate Expectations.* I am not sure what I was able to contribute, but I learned a lot collaborating with some very committed Catholic educators. These expectations were proposed for graduates of a Catholic school:

- a discerning believer formed in the Catholic faith community
- an effective communicator
- a reflective, creative and holistic thinker
- a self-directed, responsible, lifelong learner
- a collaborative contributor

- a caring family member
- a responsible citizen

In 2011, the graduate expectations were reviewed and renewed. To be sure, these expectations are idealistic, and yet they are so important as a guideline and a critique of practice. But this week has not been a good week for graduates of Catholic schools. A graduate of a Catholic high school is accused of the mass killing of students in Calgary; a graduate of a Catholic high school in London is charged with hacking into the Canada Revenue Agency; and in a suburban Toronto Catholic high school, students were arrested for knife attacks. I don't believe I would have made the Catholic school connection in these three examples of moral failing had they not all occurred within a couple of days, with newspaper accounts all referring to the Catholic connection. Every Catholic educator knows that sin is pretty plentiful in one's workplace and community. The adult animators and the student learners are very human, and are developing in their faith and in the ways they live love. While there is a whole lot of love and grace in our Catholic school communities, there is also more than a little anger and pride and selfishness.

It is always disappointing when something egregiously sinful happens in a Catholic school. Indeed, it is an invitation for us to realize that we do everything from humility. We need that humility in every aspect of what we are about. We are not there yet—far from it. But moral failing is something we learn to deal with. Especially in sin we can find rich gospel lessons of forgiveness and of a call to change. Three high-profile failures of living the gospel should not in any way diminish our gospel enthusiasm or compromise how we look at our graduate expectations. If anything, all of the partners in Catholic education—parents, teachers, administrators and parish priests—should become even more aware of the high standards we have set for the Catholic education of children. And with awareness should come sharper imagination about the different situations during the school year when we can reinforce one or another of the expectations.

April 18—Good Friday

During Holy Week, classes come to the school auditorium to attend a dramatic way of the cross performed in tableau form by a high school troupe. On Good Friday evening, the student actors come to the church. This has been part of Good Friday here in the parish for more than 20 years. Usually about 100 to 150 people come for this prayer. It is always very much appreciated in the parish.

April 20—Easter Sunday

Baptisms of the RCIC Children

Easter Sunday, as always, has been extraordinary here in the parish, as I am sure it is in every parish. A Sunday full of joy! So many attending all of our Masses. So many hands shaken and "Happy Easter!" greetings given. Most of the First Communion children participated at one or another of our Easter Masses with their families. The families sought out the balloons in the foyer, and the name of each First Communicant present was read out to great applause before Mass ended.

At 2:00 p.m. we celebrated the special Eucharist with Baptism for the ten RCIC children. The children's excitement was palpable. Godparents were present, along with family members. Yet, at the end of Mass, I felt some disappointment. Not with the children, but with the Catholic adults in their lives. Many of them seemed lost during the liturgy, not aware of when to sit or stand or kneel, and not knowing the responses. They were more fixed on their cellphone cameras. In reviewing this Mass, I arrived at two conclusions. First, these are parents who want Baptism for their children so that their children can receive Holy Communion with their classmates. I hope that it is more than this, but that much seems clear. Second, in the future, we might have to insist on a practice session, walking children, parents and extended family members through the Easter Baptism liturgy as it will unfold, and working with the adults on how to respond by using the Mass cards. Of course, this will have to be done with pastoral sensitivity, but formation is in order. My hope is that it will be a moment of some faith ownership and faith development for the parents and other adults present. Miracles still do happen at Easter!

April 23—Easter Week

Easter Mass for the Schools

This week, the elementary school communities will come to the church for Eucharist. The program is pretty well set now. The principals begin by speaking of the power of Easter for Christians, and remind the students why it is good for the Catholic school community to celebrate a school Mass at Eastertime. The readings chosen for the Mass are accessed from the *Green Binder*, and the intercessions are prepared by the school. The parish musicians have visited the schools and practised with the school choirs for the liturgy. The readers who are chosen generally are very good. They have practised. Best of all, they can be understood. We remind the readers of the older people who are here at the school Mass, some of their parents and grandparents, who have failing ears. It is important to read loudly and slowly for them. The students get the message. Students in Grade 5 and up can do good liturgical proclamation. (Exceptionally, one might have great readers from the lower grades. Indeed, this is usually the case for the class First Communion Mass. This week, one of the schools, to incorporate the very young students and make them feel important, had some of the little ones serve as readers. The idea was laudable, but it did not make for good liturgy, as the reading was unintelligible. The focus was directed at the children, not on the Word of God proclaimed.) The Easter week school Mass is an opportune time for a brief homily to trace Jesus' trip from Good Friday to the resurrection on Easter Sunday and to explore what the resurrection means for us, Jesus' followers, today.

Culturally, as we know, Easter plays second fiddle to Christmas. The children are immersed in all of the cultural and commercial trappings of Christmas, yet some of the Christmas biblical essentials do stick with the children, along with all of the frills. Such is not the case with Easter. Pope Francis touches on this cultural crisis as it affects the family:

> The family is experiencing a profound cultural crisis, as are all communities and social bonds. In the case of the family, the weakening of these bonds is particularly serious because the family is the fundamental cell of society, where we learn to live with others despite our differences and to belong to one another; it is also the place where parents pass on the faith to their children. (*The Joy of the Gospel*, 66)

Easter is the core and the liturgical centrepiece of our faith. Yet, sadly, more than a few families fail to pass on the Easter faith to their children during their Easter dinners and celebrations. There is little or no reference to the resurrection of Jesus, our Lord and Saviour. The Easter story is not told to the children. Thus, the Easter school Mass becomes the privileged moment for the Easter story to be told and the Risen Christ celebrated with the community.

April 27

The Class Celebration of First Communion

Today, at a special Sunday afternoon Eucharist, the Grade 2 children from one of the schools had their first "formal" Holy Communion. (We call this their "formal" First Communion because the children have already celebrated their First Communion on Easter Sunday with their families.) Celebrations for the other two schools will take place in Sundays to come.

The class First Communion includes extended family members and friends in attendance. On the Friday before First Communion Sunday, the children come to the church for their practice. And a couple of weeks before that, our music ministry, along with the teachers, spent time with each class, teaching them the songs and responses.

Before the Mass, we make the usual announcement asking folks to silence their cellphones and pagers, to refrain from chewing gum and drinking their bottled water, and to use their photo-taking devices only at the end of the liturgy. We do our best to create as holy an environment as possible.

The children process into the church wearing their white First Communion robes, and take their place. Father Vijay is very welcoming to the children and to the large assembly. The readers are excellent, loud and clear, and it is most heartening to hear the children respond so boldly to Father Vijay's dialogue prayer with them. A collection is taken at each First Communion. Before the Mass, I explain that the money collected will be directed to our food bank, St. Vincent de Paul ministry and Harvest Kitchen (our soup kitchen). The children bring the collection to the altar with the gifts at the offertory. We pray Eucharistic Prayer II for Children. For the Liturgy of the Eucharist, the children come into the sanctuary around the altar, and they continue to sing enthusiastically the responses to the different invocations in this prayer. This Eucharistic Prayer for Children is a beautiful and meaningful prayer that everyone can understand. And it is still happily untouched by the Vatican makeover!

At Communion time, the teachers on either side of Father Vijay direct each child as he or she receives Jesus in the Eucharist. The children are congratulated before the final blessing and enjoy the applause of the assembly. In turn, the gift of the children to their families and friends is a great little action song (a hymn choreographed with arm and hand movements) that they perform before the final procession.

May 2

Meeting of the Local Catholic Education Alliance Committee

The second meeting of the renewed Catholic Education Alliance Committee took place today. It was a noon-hour meeting that lasted close to two hours. This is a large committee, with representation from every sector of the Catholic education partners and from society at large. The co-chairs are the bishop and the chair of the board.

The director of education serves as chair of the meeting. There was a lively discussion around the theme of making the case for the legitimacy and the necessity of our Catholic schools. The discussion took on a sharper focus when news was conveyed during the meeting that there will be a provincial election on June 12. The news of the election reinforced the urgency of the task of making our case with the public. The board will produce a fact sheet and a list of talking points for encounters with members of the provincial parliament and candidates for the different parties. Parishes will be contacted with bulletin announcements asking Catholics to be sure that they are listed as Catholic school supporters on the voters' lists.

MAY 4

Education Week

Serving in the Love of Christ. This is the theme for this year's Catholic Education Week. At each Mass this weekend, a student from one of our schools reads an announcement on the meaning of Catholic Education Week. The message expressed: great thanks for publicly funded Catholic schools; an appreciation of the close ties between parish and school; the faith foundation students receive through a Catholic education; a recognition of past sacrifices that made today's Catholic education possible. The message concludes by encouraging parishioners to be sure that they are registered as Catholic school supporters.

MAY 6

Begin Preparing for the Sacrament of Confirmation to Take Place in November

This is a short visit, less than half an hour, to meet with the Grade 7 students who will celebrate Confirmation in November. We begin in late spring, because the sacrament itself takes place in the fall. The summer months lessen our contacts with the candidates. With each student, the teachers have already sent home letters from

the parish announcing a meeting that will take place the week of May 20 for Confirmation candidates, their parents and sponsors. A copy of the letter is included in the *Green Binder*. The letter makes it clear that the sacrament of Confirmation is a parish experience, not a school event.

The intention of this visit is catechesis. I want to assure the students (and I tell them that from now on they will be called "candidates") that Confirmation is their choice. Their parents made the choice for them at Baptism. Now this is the moment for them to say "yes" to their Baptism—that is, if they want to! I also talk about the meaning of the sacrament and some of the elements involved in preparing for Confirmation. Caitlyn, in the front row of one of the classes, comes to my aid. Caitlyn was baptized in St. Michael's Ukrainian Church, which means that she is already confirmed. This is a chance to present Confirmation as a sacrament of initiation: in the Eastern rites, the three sacraments of initiation happen at the same liturgy. Other students in the class are surprised that Caitlyn also received First Communion at her Baptism (for infants, communion is given as a few drops of consecrated wine). Caitlyn will journey with the other candidates towards Confirmation, as this will be an intentional time for her to grow in her faith. And at the Confirmation liturgy, she will receive a blessing from the bishop.

I underline the importance of the meeting for candidates and parents, to make the official request for the sacrament and to form or educate the parents themselves, to offer them an understanding of Confirmation. I share with the candidates the date for a second get-together, the occasion for the Rite of Acceptance at the Eucharist we will have on June 4 for all of the candidates for Confirmation, their parents and the sponsors who are able to be present.

May 7

Education Week Student Trustee Mass

And now for something completely different! Today, in the middle of Catholic Education Week, at the same time across Ontario, the Eucharist was celebrated in each Catholic high school to give thanks for the gift of publicly funded Catholic education and to storm heaven in prayer for faithful continuation of Catholic education in our province. This was an initiative of the provincial Catholic Student Trustees' Association. I was asked to preside at the Eucharist. It was a special experience.

For the first time in a long time, the entire student body was present for Mass at the same time. Usually, because of numbers, two Masses are needed for the high school. But in the second semester, there are fewer students, and a pair of portable bleachers was recently acquired, seating 150 persons per bleacher. The portable bleachers fit nicely on each side of the gym. Amazingly, with the permanent bleachers, chairs and the portable bleachers, all 1200 students plus faculty were seated for the Eucharist. The choir was enhanced with the addition of a half dozen boys who came on the scene from their starring roles in the school musical, *Joseph and the Amazing Technicolor Dreamcoat.*

There are two points to make about the participation of this liturgical assembly: the staff and students were very focused, so there was very little fussing or distractedness; also, predictably, the responses, save for the choir, were muted at best. That seems to be endemic to adolescents everywhere. What a contrast with the kids at the First Communion Mass a few days ago!

I felt that this occasion allowed me to get serious with the assembly about the enduring gift of Catholic education. I related in the penitential rite that I want to do more than simply say the "Lord, have mercy," often mouthed with little thought or meaning. So I asked God's mercy and forgiveness as I identified some of the sins of the students: bullying, mockery, demeaning, cheating and plagiarism, abuse and self-abuse, trashing and disrespect of the environment. And I asked God's mercy and forgiveness for the sins of the teachers: paying lip-service to their vocation as Catholic educator, hypocrisy, laziness and going through the motions, sarcasm and verbal abuse. And I asked God's mercy on the sin of the entire school community: taking for granted the gift that is ours in Catholic education.

The readings from scripture are the readings of the day, an Easter weekday, a Wednesday. I felt compelled to give a word of introduction for each of the readings. Few in the assembly would be able to plug into Saul, the martyrdom of Stephen and then Philip leaving Jerusalem and going off to Samaria. If folks are going to hear the Word, they at least need a context to understand the Word.

The homily was brief. I simply asked those present to get inside their memory bank and to revisit some of the precious moments and experiences that have made up their Catholic education, moments that are consistent with and specific to our mission and that would not take place in a school of our public board. I guided them to return to their First Communion and Reconciliation and Confirmation. It is in Reconciliation that personal conscience is awakened and begins to take shape. I asked them to get in touch with the way they pray, how they were taught to pray, and what prayer means for them today. And to trace the development of their social conscience and the opening up of their private worlds to others in the form of service: food drives, fair trade club, the walk against violence against women, the sacredness of our environment, and development projects visited in Peru and the Dominican Republic and supported through the Pilgrimage experience. I invited them to keep in mind that the learning that happens here is in a faith community, with Christ as the centre of our mission. Another form of service includes counselling—the support given in time of personal and family crisis. A community of caring teachers is the glue of the Catholic school community and the personal relationships established.

Behind all of this is the thought of Pope Francis: "Catholic schools, which always strive to join their work of education with the explicit proclamation of the Gospel, are a most valuable resource for the evangelization of culture" (*The Joy of the Gospel,* 134).

May 8

The Return of Konrad!

He's back! *The Globe and Mail* today presents Konrad Yakabuski—the sequel. And today he seems really annoyed. Today his banner title is "Ontario Catholic Schools are more contradictory than ever." As we have been celebrating Catholic Education Week so, too, does Konrad refer to Catholic Education Week, to the provincial election and to his frustration that the issue of Catholic school funding will likely not be raised during the election, unless it is raised by the Green Party.

He sounds a lot like a postmodern secular prophet wailing in the wilderness. He is really fixed on sex, it seems: that is, homosexuality. Catholic schools discriminate, he says. Catholic schools indoctrinate with their religion courses, he adds. And he wonders why, in light of such blatant discrimination, indoctrination and duplication of funding, do so many non-Catholic parents continue to send their children to Catholic schools?

The sad thing is that he has such superficial understanding of what Catholic education is all about. Surely there has to be something good and positive about Catholic education! But Konrad fails to get at the mystery of why Catholic education has stood the test of time. The way he goes on, I doubt that he even tries to look deeper into what we are about. That, it seems to me, is shoddy journalism. I want to ask, "Konrad, is there anything good about Catholic schools? Do you think that the quality of our academics has anything to do with a faith-based learning environment? Why do so many of the kids in our schools seem so happy? Why do so many of our students appreciate religion class and chaplaincy teams? Why is community spirit a hallmark at just about every Catholic school? Can't a faith-centred world view impact on literature and the ways we do politics and economics?" In Konrad's postmodern secular view of religion, Jesus and faith and gospel and mission seem to be non-factors.

But, secular prophet that he is, he does have a point, and it would be foolish of us not to pay heed. The existence of publicly funded Catholic education is always going to be questioned. He represents the point of view that there is great suspicion in the land in our very secular times concerning the legitimacy of a Catholic institution receiving public funds. He also articulates quite passionately the tenets of the secular religion, a religion that is making greater and

greater inroads into the thinking and the responses of our fellow citizens today. The questions I ask of Konrad Yakabuski above are the questions that we must work to answer ourselves to demonstrate that publicly financed Catholic schools really do make a difference to the quality of life in Ontario.

May 8

Grade 7 Retreat in the Parish Hall

This week, our youth ministry team is collaborating with the schools and the Grade 7 teacher and students for a day-long retreat in the parish hall. Each school has a retreat day, which makes the process very manageable. The theme of the day is forgiveness. Students explore the theme through exercises, crafts, a video, time for personal reflection, group sharing and creating. Students are invited to identify in a symbolic way their own personal luggage that they would like to throw out. They work at creating a prayer asking the Holy Spirit to help them forgive and let go. These prayers become part of the Mass. The class Mass takes place in the church. The scripture readings are chosen to continue a reflection on God's forgiveness through Jesus. The small-group intimacy of the Mass is special for the students, as it allows for gentle teaching reminders on the parts of the Mass—what the liturgy of the Word is … the liturgy of the Eucharist … the Eucharistic Prayer … the calling of the Holy Spirit to come upon the gifts … the appeal to the Lamb of God for forgiveness.

May 15

Partners in Catholic Education

Each spring, the school board organizes a gathering of principals, parents and parish priests around a meal. (There is something very Catholic about the Catholic school board and its appreciation or strategy of doing things around a meal!) The event is called, appropriately enough, Partners in Catholic Education, and the purpose is just that—to bring the partners together, making real, at least for an evening, the triad of home, school and parish. There were more than 300 persons in attendance. Along with the meal, there is always some animation or formation. This evening, Father Thomas Rosica, CSB, the founder and CEO of Salt and Light Television, gave the keynote address. Father Rosica, a polished communicator, was in great form. He demonstrated quickly that he knew his audience. He was able to affirm them in their common vocation of Catholic educator and in their common love for Catholic education. And then he shared with them anecdotes of his media work, especially with the Vatican. The core of his message, though, was the extraordinary impact that Pope Francis continues to have both within and outside the church. According to Father Rosica, for Pope Francis, it is always grace and mercy over strictness; we are to be a church of the heart and are to minister in the periphery, rather than the centre—that is, our ministry belongs with the voiceless and powerless rather than with the powerful elite. These are themes that surface frequently in the pope's apostolic exhortation on *The Joy of the Gospel*. In conclusion, Father Rosica left this question with the assembled partners: "Are we as a Catholic school system in Ontario capable of warming people's hearts?"

May 20–22: A busy three days in May!

Formal Reconciliation for Grade 3s

In Grade 3, we prepare the children for their first formal Reconciliation. In Grade 2, we offered a brief experience of confession for the children before First Communion. Back in February, we hosted an evening for the parents of the Grade 3 children to help them undertake the formation of their children. At that meeting, we equipped the parents with a copy of *We Prepare for Reconciliation* (Novalis, 2010). This is the same excellent text that the teachers use in the classroom.

Now the time has arrived for the children's formal Reconciliation. Each school is given an evening. The parents who are interested and who want this sacrament for their children bring them to the church. (This is about 85 percent of the parents.) The teachers are present to assist. Two weeks before the Reconciliation evening, Father Vijay visited each class to answer questions and to review the liturgy. He explained the parables of mercy, so the children are well prepared. The liturgy unfolds beautifully, with a welcoming hymn sung by the children. The PowerPoint on the screen presents the gospel: the story of the Good Shepherd seeking out the one sheep that was lost. The children lead the communal examination of conscience. There are two priests seated in a corner of the sanctuary for Confession. Teachers escort each child to a priest. After each child has made his or her Confession, there is a common penance: the group prays together the Our Father. The liturgy concludes with a hymn, and then the teachers present a certificate to each child, a souvenir of his or her First Formal Reconciliation. (At our formation session with the parents, we presented a catechesis on the beauty and power of the sacrament of Reconciliation. We insisted that this sacrament is for everyone and invited them to participate. Indeed, the catechesis was directed at the adults. Very few take up that invitation. Why? This is a mystery that begs to be understood.)

First Confirmation Meeting for Candidates, Parents and Sponsors

As the Grade 3s are celebrating Reconciliation in the church, downstairs in the hall we begin the formation process for Confirmation with the Grade 7s. As mentioned earlier, the sacrament itself does not take place until mid-November, but we do need to begin the preparation before the summer. I have gone to the Grade 7 classes and presented the idea of Confirmation to the students. At each of the three schools, I stress that I speak to them as candidates for Confirmation from St. Kevin's parish community, not so much as students from a particular school. The sacrament of Confirmation is a parish experience, not a school activity. We have already asked the schools to send the Catholic parents a letter of invitation to gather for an initial meeting on this date. (A copy of the letter is found in the *Green Binder*.) Sponsors are also invited to the initial meeting.

Over the three evenings, most candidates and parents are present. Of about 100 candidates, fewer than ten did not respond. This is par for the course. We will issue a further invitation to these parents and candidates to meet with us. No response to that invitation means they are not interested.

The agenda for the meeting is to have parents make the formal request for the sacrament of Confirmation. As well, it is an opportunity to catechize the candidates and, along with them, the parents and sponsors about the meaning of Confirmation. At these meetings, there are always three challenges.

The first challenge is the level of cooperation the Grade 7 teacher is willing to render. We ask the teacher to help us identify and greet the parents and candidates, and to assist us with the paperwork. Some of the teachers are enthusiastic; they provide great assistance. But a few, by their body language and behaviour, make it clear that they would rather be anywhere else but with us. (I have often asked the principals to please try to situate their truly committed teachers in those grades in which we form the children for the sacraments. Kids, even at a tender age, can detect authenticity. They can also recognize those teachers who are simply going through the motions. In *The Joy of the Gospel*, Pope Francis reminds us: "We need to remember that all religious teaching ultimately has to be reflected in the teacher's way of life, which awakens the assent of the heart by its nearness, love and witness" [42]).

The second challenge has to do with communicating the theology of Confirmation. *Be sealed with the gift of the Holy Spirit!* The sacrament is the giving of the Holy Spirit. It is a sacrament of initiation, and it is understood by some as the sacrament marking Christian maturity. But it is also the sacrament in which the person says a resounding "yes" to his or her Baptism. In a way, it is all of the above! The catechesis we offer touches on all of these meanings.

The third challenge involves choosing an appropriate sponsor for Confirmation. We go over the criteria to be a sponsor. We suggest that candidates and parents look first to a godparent from the child's

Baptism. The sticking point for the parent and the candidate is finding someone who takes their faith seriously and works at being faithful in participating in the life of a parish. This is yet another indicator of the increasing secularization that affects Catholic culture. We ask that the sponsor chat with their parish priest, sharing that he or she has been asked to be a Confirmation sponsor, and asking the parish priest to indicate that said sponsor belongs to a parish community. In the parish, we began to formalize this process for being a sponsor, since several years earlier, we discovered on a Confirmation evening that three of the sponsors were not Catholic! We understand that this request of the sponsor might even be a moment of challenge, a time for the sponsor to look hard at her or his faith life.

The meeting ends with a reminder for our next meeting—Wednesday evening, June 4. At this celebration of the Eucharist, we will have the Rite of Acceptance. We ask that all candidates and parents be present, along with as many sponsors as are able.

Grade 6 Retreats

The Grade 6 retreats take place in the parish hall this week, during the school day. The format is similar to the retreats for the Grade 7s. Again, the retreat is the result of collaboration between our parish youth ministry team and the school, especially the Grade 6 teachers. The theme is conservation of the environment, or the integrity of creation. Students discuss what it is to be responsible stewards of the earth for future generations. The footprint symbol is central to the reflection, inviting the students to brainstorm on what they want to leave behind for future generations. In the Eucharist, the beauty and gift of creation are proclaimed in a reading from chapter 1 of the Book of Genesis. The intercessions are the collective prayers created from students' reflection on the ideas and ideals generated from their time together. A few days after the Grade 6 retreats, Pope Francis took up the theme of creation and conservation at his weekly audience: "God always forgives but Creation never forgives, and if we destroy Creation, in the end it will destroy us."

The Identifying Leadership Program

Here is a moment that is not part of our regular parish–school routine. The coordinator of staff development for the Catholic school board asked me to spend some time with the Identifying Leadership program. This group of about 25 teachers has been meeting with different mentors, reviewing aspects of administrative leadership for a Catholic school. I was with them at the outset of the program about two years ago, reflecting on some of the vision questions for Catholic education. This afternoon is their final session together, and I was invited for a further reflection on leadership in the Catholic school. Given that we are now in the middle of a provincial election, and the question of continued existence for our Catholic schools always seems to come up during an election, I thought that if we are to have any future at all as a publicly financed school system in an increasingly secularized society, we must reinforce the question of Catholic identity for present and future leaders. My remarks centred on the imperative of having a passion for the mission of Catholic education and a knowledge of the story of what it is to be a Catholic Christian. I stressed that the knowledge of the story be a knowledge that leaders are prepared to share. Inevitably, I had to touch on their need to live their faith and be open to growing in their faith, and added that they cannot do that as an individual apart from the praying and worshipping Christian community. Leaders can do all the visioning and strategizing for the Catholic education project they want, but unless they pray regularly with a community, they are building their Catholic house on sand.

With the participants, I referred to the Canadian bishops' December 2013 document entitled *The Essential Elements of Evangelization Today*. The bishops observe that our present culture is marked by a deep pluralism and that our situation of proclaiming the gospel today is not unlike that of the early Christians, who evangelized in cultures of different religions and philosophical traditions. As a method for evangelization, the bishops propose a strong emphasis in word and deed on *witness, community* and *service*. In the Reflection section of this Journal (see Reflection 1, "The Shifting

Sands of Publicly Funded Catholic Education in Canada"), I develop at some length the challenge of maintaining Catholic identity in our pluralistic, secular culture.

June 3—Feast of St. Kevin

Staff Mass

The feast day of our parish patron is June 3. St. Kevin's life, if we believe the many legends, spanned the sixth century. He was a hermit who became an abbot and a very influential spiritual and intellectual leader of the church in Ireland. That much is true. In 1951, the founding pastor of the parish, who was of Irish descent, was influential in choosing the name "Kevin" as patron. As we have four Catholic schools attached to St. Kevin's parish, it seemed natural several years ago to invite the Catholic educators in the schools to gather on the feast of St. Kevin for Eucharist and some hospitality. We do so at day's end, about 3:45 p.m., with a certain amount of trepidation, as we are asking "one more thing" from our teachers. But generally, we get a good response. And to be honest, it is more than us asking one more thing from them; indeed, they are receiving from us, from the parish, affirmation in their mission and nourishment for their ministry. Each year, about half of the Catholic educators in our parish schools (90 to 100) are able to participate in this Eucharist with us. Each school does have a significant presence, which is important, as it underlines the unity of our faith education mission in the parish.

We do not rush through Mass, but we are aware of the time, and we schedule for 45 minutes. Volunteers from each school assist in the liturgy. The readings selected speak to the need for unity of purpose, coming away for a little while, and mission. The brief homily is a thank-you from the parish, a recognition of the unity of the evangelizing ministry that we share in the four schools, and encouragement to go deeper into the meaning of their Baptism.

JUNE 4

Confirmation Preparation—Eucharist and Rite of Acceptance

The period of formation leading to the sacrament of Confirmation roughly follows the framework of the Rite of Christian Initiation of Adults. We celebrate three moments with a ritual: The Rite of Acceptance, the Rite of Enrolment and the Rite of Commitment. This evening we celebrated the first of these rituals. (Recall that the second and third rituals are celebrated in the fall in preparation for Confirmation in November.) We do the Rite of Acceptance within the context of the Eucharist. This year, the liturgical and spiritual environment for the Mass is enhanced by the closeness of the feast of Pentecost and by references to the Holy Spirit in the prayers of the Mass.

The candidates were present with their parents and, if possible, their sponsors. After the homily, candidates were called to the sanctuary to receive the covenant with the parish community, which was signed the evening they requested the sacrament. Representing the parish community, our pastor, Father Vijay, also signed each of the covenants. As well, candidates received a red booklet containing the texts of the Creed, the Gifts of the Holy Spirit, the Fruits of the Holy Spirit and the Confirmation Prayer. Speaking for the parish, the Grade 7 teachers presented the candidates, indicated that they were ready to begin preparing for the sacrament, and asked the parish to assist them in their further formation. I accepted on behalf of the parish, and then candidates and assembly professed together the Apostles' Creed in question form, as is used in the sacrament of Baptism. For the prayers of intercession, the candidates alone prayed for the gifts of the Holy Spirit:

Spirit of Wisdom, help me to seek God.
Spirit of Understanding, enlighten my mind.
Spirit of Counsel, enlighten and guide me in all my ways.
Spirit of Fortitude, uphold my soul in every time of trouble.

Spirit of Knowledge, help me to know good from evil.
Spirit of Reverence, possess my heart.
Spirit of Wonder and Awe, penetrate my inmost heart.

Teens can be shy or wary of being uncool. The candidates are seated with parents and sponsors. At the moment of questioning—"Do you make a special choice today to enter into the process to prepare for Confirmation? Do you freely choose to work at following the teaching of Jesus in the Gospel? Do you promise to be faithful to the Covenant made with the parish?"—candidates are asked to respond, "I do!" It is not difficult, really, but their collective response is often muted. Maybe there is a formation challenge for us here: as we work with the candidates to prepare them for the Rite of Acceptance Eucharist, we can encourage them to participate boldly. After all, boldness and witness are signs of the presence of the Holy Spirit!

Adults can be shy, too. They may not have been to church for a while, and may not know the responses to the prayers. About 300 people were at the liturgy this evening, counting candidates, parents, sponsors and other family members. While we recognized a number of families who participate regularly in the worship life of the parish, there were still many families we did not know. These would be the secular or occasional Catholics. Learning from past experiences, we roped off the back pews of the church to encourage people to sit closer to the altar and ambo. This created a more intimate worshipping space. Even then, it was uncanny to observe people's automatic Catholic response to sit in the back pews. The usher kindly asked them to move up. They did so, but still they looked for the last row possible. It was fun to see the reaction of those who arrived just before the beginning of the liturgy as they trekked to the empty two front pews. They seemed anxious and mildly embarrassed. Of course, we experienced the same response with the teachers the day before ... most want to situate themselves at a great distance from the front of the church, the altar and ambo. Why this reaction? One benign interpretation might be that the Catholic in the last pew is more like the tax collector than the Pharisee—shy, humble, aware of her own sinfulness and his need of God's mercy, unworthy to go any deeper into the sacred space of the church. And I am sure there are other interpretations, both benign and less benign!

June 10–12

Closing School Mass

The end is near! Three closing school Masses over two days. To be sure, the enthusiasm is still there. Probably the elementary children are a little more hyper. But this is manageable, because the routine has set in, and coming to the church is no longer a strange new experience. One school had a very effective introduction to the liturgy, with children bringing to the altar different objects representing the year's work: books, a baseball glove, a poster depicting the school's journey through the sacraments, and a compost bin indicating that the school is environmentally friendly. For this festive occasion, we sang the clapping "Gloria." This hymn of praise is indeed joyful, and it involves everyone in the assembly. As well, the use of Eucharistic Prayer II for Children invites strong sung participation by students and teachers alike. For these school liturgies, we continue to welcome a number of parents and grandparents as well. At the end of Mass, we wished everyone well and urged them to come and see us on Sundays during July and August!

June 11

High School Graduation Mass

A large group of graduates—some 300—made the half-kilometre trek from the school to the church for the celebration of their graduation Mass. The Eucharist in the parish church is a June tradition for graduates. The liturgy was good: the choir sang well, the readers proclaimed the readings well, and the students were attentive. As usual, though, except for the choir members at their microphones, the dialogue responses with the assembly were all one-way. My "The Lord be with you" drifted off alone without any accompaniment into the ether.

In the homily, I proposed that the graduates consider concurrent time—two systems of time operating simultaneously: 24-hours-a-day time, or now time, and Holy Spirit time. I described 24-hours-a-day time: time to eat and drink and see to daily needs, to work and to save up, to work out and to celebrate and party, to make friends and lose friends, to study and plan and travel and spend hours on mindless TV shows and video games. I then proposed Holy Spirit time: time to serve and to reverence, to give back and to remember, to wonder and to discern God's purpose for your life, to embrace the cross. I concluded by saying that the challenge at every stage in life is to bring Holy Spirit time into 24-hours-a-day time or, even more, to recognize how the Holy Spirit wants to be integrated into the everydayness of our lives. I think I did well. I sure worked at it.

But I think the real homily came at the end of Mass. Tina and Paul Turner, graduates of the school, are also long-time teachers in the school, and very effective and influential teachers at that. Their middle daughter, Julia, who would have been a member of this graduating class, died of cancer at the beginning of her Grade 10 year. It was a six-month struggle for Julia, and her classmates were very much a part of that struggle. As a memorial for Julia, students in the class created a beautiful butterfly carved out of wood. The 300 members of the class signed their names on the back and presented it to Paul and Tina. It was Paul and Tina's thank-you that became the true homily: the simple eloquence of their thank-you, the way they underlined the absolute importance of a supportive community in dealing with sickness and death, and their declaration that it was their faith in Jesus that sustained them and continues to sustain them. Their boldness was remarkable as they declared to the graduates: "Faith in Jesus is everything. Always remember that!"

June 16

Planning Meeting with Principals for September

The four principals and the high school chaplaincy leader arrived at the rectory at 11:30 a.m. They were armed with their BlackBerrys and assorted agendas and timetables for the September–December term. We had prepared a draft program for them to consider: a program of collaboration between the Catholic school and the parish. This was not a new exercise. We knew from past years the important activities, dates and times that would be required. As usual, the principals were most agreeable and accommodating. I believe that, in addition to their goodwill and civility, the glass of Prosecco at the beginning of the meeting and the prospect of excellent sausage sandwiches for lunch helped clinch the principals' agreement. The September–December program would be inserted into the *Green Binder* and would become our pastoral road map for those first four months of the school year.

This meeting is a kind of affirmation of the solidarity existing between the four schools and the parish. Friendship among principals and priests is reinforced in such meetings and helps enormously in advancing the pastoral project. I find that clear planning is imperative for accomplishing our goals. In reviewing the draft program, we realized that we had to change several proposed dates because of conflicts. As well, the principals were able to offer some suggestions of their own, based on their experience in administration and their knowledge of the students. One principal remarked that now, with the dates agreed upon, she will be able to order the buses she will need from September to December to bring the students to the church for Mass. She will do that as soon as she returns to school at the end of August. Experience also tells us that the planning we do today is not written in stone; inevitably, there will be disruptions, and we will need to be flexible. Creative flexibility is a given. But, all in all, the two hours spent together in June give us a head start in dealing with the mad flurry of activity that defines the beginning of September for both school and parish.

JUNE 19

Grade 8 Graduation Mass

Up until two years ago, Grade 8 graduation was challenging. I speak here, of course, from the point of view of the parish. We would hold the exercises here in the church on three different evenings, with one evening for each school. The church would be full of parents, family and friends. The ceremony would begin with Mass. Following Mass and the removal of the Blessed Sacrament to the sacristy, the graduation exercises would take place, with brief speeches and the awarding of honours to graduates. This part of the program was accompanied by the hollering and shouts of joy that are part of graduations at all levels! At the end of the ceremony, the students and teachers would descend to the hall for pizza or a sit-down meal followed by a dance.

Two years ago we proposed a change. Our experience was that the Mass had become the *Catholic cosmetic*, something a Catholic school was expected to have at graduation time. As a parish, we wanted to separate Mass from graduation exercises in order to give more attention to the Mass. It would be a moment to focus on faith—the importance of the students' faith journey over the last eight or more years and for the next part of the journey. With the cooperation of the principals, we decided on one graduation Mass for the Grade 8s of the three schools. (For the exercises themselves, the schools take advantage of the air-conditioned auditorium at the high school, with an evening for each school.)

The Mass took place this morning. In all there were 110 graduates. The students donned their gowns (the schools had already received the graduation gowns students would wear the next week) and processed into the church to Elgar's "Pomp and Circumstance." The entrance hymn followed. The students proclaimed the Word of God, led us in the prayer of the faithful and brought the gifts to the altar. Our pastor, Father Vijay, presided and I concelebrated. We shared the homily, underscoring the message of the gospel reading from Matthew about always being ready to shoulder one's cross, and reminding them of the call of Jeremiah that age is never a factor in responding to the call to follow the Lord. The Lord calls us when we are young; the Lord calls us when we are old. The call is always there. We stressed the blessing of a Catholic education, which they have enjoyed and will continue to enjoy. We prayed for them while we stood near the baptismal font, beside the Paschal candle. We prayed that, as they journey through life, especially in the next phase of their life in high school, they may work at being the light of Christ: this is the commitment made for them at Baptism and the commitment they owned for themselves at Confirmation.

Many of the parents and family members were not present this morning. Perhaps this is the downside of having a morning graduation Mass for the graduates. We were surprised, however, by the number of family members who were able to participate with us. It is clear that next year we must send to each graduate's family an invitation from the parish to join us for the graduation Mass.

JUNE 19

Catholic Education Alliance Committee Meeting

I have arrived at the final entry of this journal. The Catholic Education Alliance Committee met today at the board office for a luncheon meeting. The session was surprisingly interesting. Several points arose:

- Prior to the provincial election last week, members of the committee had canvassed political candidates in several ridings for their views on publicly funded Catholic education. The encounters were very positive. The suggestion was made to do this again during a non-election period to see if that strong endorsement of Catholic education prevails.
- The One School System Group is a watchdog organization whose purpose is to see the demise of publicly funded Catholic schools in Ontario. We were briefed on their new strategy, in which some of their members set up shop across the street from every Catholic high school in the province to alert students that they can opt out of taking religion. This group feels that recent court decisions have gone their way. Without religion, Catholic schools would have no reason for continuing. Or so goes their reasoning. The director of education and the trustee on the committee pointed out some real flaws in these arguments.

- There was a discussion about the upcoming Pride parade in Toronto. The Ontario English Catholic Teachers' Association (OECTA) decided at its annual meeting to have a presence in the parade, given that it is a global event this year. The thinking is that the association would support students, teachers and others in the LGBT community and their right to be free of bullying and harassment. The teachers see this initiative as speaking out against discrimination. Their decision has been opposed by Parents As First Educators and by others, including Cardinal Thomas Collins, Archbishop of Toronto, who remarked that the OECTA decision is unfortunate and shows an inadequate understanding of the Catholic faith. York Catholic school board trustee Cathy Ferlisi, quoted in the *Toronto Star* on June 17, 2014, said that "The parade was not an appropriate venue as it would have partially clad participants, acts of nudity and simulated sexual activities. She stated that the parade is not congruent with Catholic teaching" (Joel Eastwood, "Catholic School Boards Debate Teachers' Pride Participation"). The Catholic Education Alliance Committee learned that some school boards have been very critical of the OECTA decision, while other Catholic school boards have simply recognized that this is an OECTA issue. My sense is that most members of the committee are not comfortable with the OECTA decision. But the OECTA member of the committee was respectful and clear in her explanation of why the teachers are doing what they are doing. To be sure, it is a divisive issue, and demonstrates the changing face of Canadian Catholicism. Maybe this is a case of black and white melding into grey.
- Several concerns were raised about the quality of religion teaching, the competence of religion teachers at the secondary level, and the attention or lack of attention given to teaching religion in elementary schools. One thoughtful member of the committee observed that at the high school level, in too many instances, assigning religion classes to teachers is often an afterthought and a convenient way to assign a class to a teacher who needs a class to teach. I sympathize with her, as

that observation resonates very much with my 30-year experience as a religion department teacher and head. I have noted elsewhere in this journal my disappointment at times with elementary teachers who have little or no passion for teaching religion and witnessing to our faith being charged with sacramental preparation. It was good that this question was raised and put on the table for future meetings.

- Finally, the director proposed that the committee consider the value of the board hosting a congress on Catholic education in the coming year. He was only able to sketch what such an event might look like, but it would involve extensive planning. Possibly it would begin on a Friday evening and take place for most of Saturday, and would involve all the partners in Catholic education, especially representation from the parishes. As we were close to adjournment, he asked us for a thought or two about such an endeavour. Not being shy, and having journeyed with Pope Francis and *The Joy of the Gospel* for most of the year in this journal, I suggested that such a congress might be a very rich moment to share Pope Francis' apostolic exhortation with many friends of Catholic education and to explore how relevant *The Joy of the Gospel* is for the evangelization we work at in our parishes and in our schools. Pope Francis states,

  > An authentic faith—which is *never* comfortable or completely personal—always involves a deep desire to change the world, to transmit values, to leave this earth somehow better than when we found it. We love this magnificent planet on which God has put us, and we love the human family, which dwells here, with all its tragedies and struggles, its hopes and aspirations, its strengths and weaknesses. The earth is our common home and all of us are brothers and sisters. If indeed "the just ordering of society and of the state is a central responsibility of politics" the Church "cannot and must not remain on the sidelines in the fight for justice". All Christians, their pastors included, are called to show concern for the building of a better world. (*The Joy of the Gospel*, 183)

Looking Back: A Concluding Word

I began this journal as a personal exercise to document the different moments when the parish community and the Catholic school collaborate in the faith education of the young Catholics in our parish. I began with the knowledge that as a parish, we have worked hard to take advantage of the Catholic schools in the parish, both for the faith education of the students and as a point of contact to be present to many parents who do not participate regularly in the parish. Recording these experiences allows me to review how we go about collaboration and to discover missed opportunities or strategies that could be changed so we can be even more effective.

In the early days of keeping the journal, I reached a moment when I thought that others might be interested in our parish–Catholic school program as a working model. Our approach is but one way of doing things, one model. It is simply a snapshot of a unique working model for a particular period of time. Maybe some of what we do and the way we do it might be helpful for others. Depending on circumstances, a parish community can choose from a range of approaches when it comes to relating to the Catholic school. This journal reflects a model that makes sense for us and that we find practical and doable. We are two priests with a very competent administrative assistant, and as religious priests, we have a supportive community of our priests close by.

Our context shapes so much of what we are able to do in collaboration with our Catholic schools. Welland is a small city in southern Ontario that has been severely hit by the economic crises of the last couple of decades. Factories have closed. Jobs are few and far between. There are many food banks and soup kitchens—too many, because they reflect the need and poverty of our citizens. The economic environment does influence our social context.

The local Catholic school board serving the Niagara Peninsula has about 23,000 students. The school board, largely due to the friendly relationship between the bishop and the director of education, cooperates very well with the diocese of St. Catharines. The school board is very supportive of the evangelization project of the parishes.

The principals we work with are friendly and accommodating. I can say the same thing for most of the teachers. A core group of teachers really do see their job more in keeping with the ministry attached to their baptismal priesthood than with their salary. Their emphasis on vocation is evident in the faith witness they live and give.

In reviewing the entries to this journal, I draw four firm conclusions:

- We have a great gift in our Catholic schools, especially in the quality of many of our educators. Baptism, by its nature, sets aside the Christian to serve as priest, prophet and king. It is this threefold baptismal character that we must acknowledge and help to form and support in our challenging postmodern culture. As a church, we still tend to be very clerical, and too often fail to encourage and endorse laypeople, such as Catholic teachers, in their ministry. Perhaps this is because priests are not always sure how to invite and include the laity in pastoral ministry.
- The students in our schools and their families reflect the changing face of Canadian Catholicism. The Catholic faith continues to mean something to the families who send their children to our schools. That "something" has wide latitude. For some, it means a great deal for their children to be educated in a faith community with Jesus Christ as the focal point of the mission of the Catholic school. Some like the fact that their children will be taught certain values. At the other end of the spectrum, some just feel that, because they are Catholic, this is what they should do. For some, living their Catholic faith means participating regularly in Sunday Eucharist; for others, it may mean volunteering at the local food bank or serving a hot supper in the soup kitchen, with less regular Sunday participation. And then there are those who would never miss Mass at Christmas and Easter. But they are all Catholics. And their children are Catholic, too.

- The new evangelization is understood in different ways. In countries such as Canada, which have been evangelized for centuries, the new evangelization tends to be understood as the means and the moment to re-evangelize, to make contact again with people whose fervour for the gospel has diminished in our aggressively secularized culture. For jurisdictions in Canada fortunate enough to have publicly financed Catholic education, the Catholic school can be a *locus pastoralis*, a place to connect with Catholics, to extend hospitality and to sensitively invite them to get in touch again with the faith that is theirs, and to discover, as if for the first time, the power and the beauty of the Catholic Christian tradition.
- Almost every entry in this journal touches on faith and prayer. That is the case because the Catholic school works at doing education in a faith community, and because the mission of the Catholic school cannot be understood apart from the mission of the Church: to proclaim Jesus as Lord and to invite students and families to discover the gospel as the blueprint for them to design and organize their lives. I am convinced that, if one is to be faithful to the mission and purpose of Catholic education, the principal actors—teachers and administrators and trustees and priests—must take seriously their Catholic faith and must work at growing in that faith. One can't really lead in prayer if one does not pray. One can't really educate in the faith if one does not work at understanding and applying one's faith to one's life. A house built on sand will not last. I would love to include here as main players all the parents of the children in our schools. In an ideal world, we would be able to do that. In our contemporary Catholic education world, most parents depend on teachers and parish to assist them or to do the faith education of their children for them. But as I note above, the schools do provide the jumping-off point for us to connect with the parents.

Finally, I can say that keeping this journal made me think: about the content of the faith education we in the parish can provide with the Catholic school, and about how we might do faith education more effectively. Often my guiding questions were "What is it we are doing and why are we doing this? And where is Jesus in all of this?" In a way, I think this process was about my faith seeking understanding, or *fides querens intellectum*, as St. Anselm defined theology. Thinking is important. It saves us from the rut of mindless habit, and it opens up new possibilities. I work at such thinking in the reflections that constitute Part II of this book.

I'd like to give the last word to Pope Francis:

> Lay people are, put simply, the vast majority of the People of God. The minority—ordained ministers—are at their service. There has been a growing awareness of the identity and mission of the laity in the Church. We can count on many lay persons, although still not nearly enough, who have a deeply rooted sense of community and great fidelity to the tasks of charity, catechesis and the celebration of the faith. At the same time, a clear awareness of this responsibility of the laity, grounded in their baptism and confirmation, does not appear in the same way in all places. In some cases, it is because lay persons have not been given the formation needed to take on important responsibilities. In others, it is because in their particular Churches room has not been made for them to speak and act, due to an excessive clericalism, which keeps them away from decision-making. (*The Joy of the Gospel*, 102)

PART II

PASTORAL REFLECTIONS ON THE GIFTS AND CHALLENGES OF CATHOLIC EDUCATION

INTRODUCTION

Why These Reflections?

About two months into keeping this journal, I began to see a pattern of sorts. Certain themes kept returning in different contexts. Through some journal entries, I was able to offer occasional commentary on particular themes, but I always had the feeling that there was more to say. Part II—Pastoral Reflections on the Gifts and Challenges of Catholic Education—provides me with the time and space to develop in more depth reflections on some of the realities we must deal with in contemporary Catholic education. I do this compelled by the urgency of which I wrote in the introduction to the journal.

There is a certain logic to the reflections I offer here. I proceed by considering the very reason for the existence of publicly financed Catholic education and how the question of our existence is facing new challenges. From a consideration of the existential reality, I move to mission and the imperative of collaboration between school and parish. In sharing that mission, we can best complement one another and work at the new evangelization, connecting with secularized Catholics in some very creative ways. For the missionary journey, the partner in Catholic education needs sustenance and encouragement. I then propose elements of spirituality that I hope will help the Catholic educator in her teaching and in his care for the students entrusted to us in our Catholic schools. The soul itself must be educated and formed in an ongoing way. Given our challenging secular, pluralistic context, what do we want to do in the Catholic education we are proposing? What can we offer our students so that their Catholic education will stick well into the future? In this reflection, I offer a strategy on fostering and helping grow *a Catholic imagination* for our students, beginning in their early years with us. Instilling awareness of and taking advantage of symbols and experiences, seasons and celebrations is so important, and can be very effective in transmitting to students the uniqueness of our Catholic tradition and in helping them in their encounter with Jesus. Finally, I offer a ten-point list of values or attitudes (I call them "principles") that I find to be very effective for evangelizing in our contemporary context. When you think about it, the context really does shape how we go about evangelizing. In the new missionary context in which we find ourselves, these principles can be helpful in building awareness and supporting practice in the Catholic education project.

I do see a gift dimension and a challenge dimension to each of the themes I explore in this section. Gift and challenge compel us to go further and to do more. Gift motivates us to not take for granted but to deepen our appreciation of the enduring legacy that is Catholic education; challenge propels us to abandon our complacency and do the hard thinking and doing needed to ensure the future of publicly funded Catholic education.

REFLECTION 1

The Shifting Sands of Publicly Funded Catholic Education in Ontario

or

Navigating the Slippery Secular Slope: Surviving in an Uncertain Social and Political Climate

In my journal entry of January 23, I referenced the op-ed piece in *The Globe and Mail* by Konrad Yakabuski: "Chapter and verse, Catholic school funding's unfair." On May 8, I referred to Yakabuski's "Ontario Catholic schools are more contradictory than ever." The usual reflex for the Ontario Catholic education community vis-à-vis the larger political life of the province is to remain low-key, to do anything but draw attention to ourselves. We fought the constitutional battles and won. We want to avoid public questioning. We simply want to be left alone to get on with doing the Catholic education project. A few years ago, in the October 2007 provincial election, we had a scare. Because the focus during that campaign was on funding for faith-based schools, public Catholic education could not avoid the collateral damage of critique on the part of the secular media, civil liberties groups and the always active lobby for the extermination of public Catholic education.

Since 2007, media articles critical of Catholic funding and vitriolic letters to the editor protesting "the Catholic privilege" have been few and far between. But it is always an unquiet peace! Konrad Yakabuski's articles, the subsequent letters to the editor in support of his position, and an online poll inviting agreement or disagreement with funding for Catholic schools indicate that anger at the Catholic entitlement to public funds for their schools continues to exist, bubbling just below the surface.

One might say that this is the mantra of some faith communities: "If we can't have public financing for our schools, then the Catholics should not have funding for their schools." Meanwhile, the mantra of the secular media proclaims that "All publicly financed education must be secular; faith and religious education belong in the home or church, synagogue and mosque, not in a public institution such as education." In 2007, the commentator Haroon Siddiqui phrased it in this way: "We have less religiosity in public discourse and in policy, the only major anomaly being the funding to Catholic schools. That, too, is now up for debate—no longer a sacred cow" (*Toronto Star*, October 4, 2007). And in 2014, in his January 23 article, Konrad Yakabuski wrote: "The principal reason Ontario should do away with Catholic school funding is not financial. There is simply no longer a case to fully fund a sectarian education system whose teachings are at odds with the fundamental values of Ontario society." His case in point: the Catholic system's resistance to gay-straight alliances.

I believe that a paradigm shift is under way in the social circumstances that provide the context for public Catholic schools in Ontario. I see some major shifts taking place, both within the tent of Catholic education and outside the tent, in the public domain. There is a new force to the argument to do away with publicly financed Catholic schools, and there are some unsettling signs in the lived reality of contemporary Catholic education. It is wise and prudent for partners in Catholic education to be aware of these present challenges. Awareness is always the beginning of any survival strategy. My hope is that this assessment of the shifting sands might sharpen the conversations on our enduring gift of Catholic education—conversations that must be ongoing if we are serious about our stewardship.

Appreciating the Shift

To appreciate what has changed in the recent past in the context of challenging or defending Catholic education, perhaps it is best for clarity's sake to spend a few moments reviewing "the lay of the land," the current state of public Catholic education. Already in the actual—in the way things are in our present situation—one can discern signs of change. The following is my personal assessment.

1. The anti-Catholic education lobby remains—although fuelled with new energy.
2. The Canadian Civil Liberties Association lobby continues to be the watchdog for secular ideology.
3. There is still a segment of the population that might be called anti-Catholic.
4. In Ontario, enrolment is declining overall. This can tempt competing boards to be increasingly aggressive when it comes to recruitment.
5. Some public and Catholic school boards and some public and Catholic teachers' unions legitimately fear the negative impact of declining enrolment and loss of jobs.
6. Some Catholic boards, for the sake of numbers (i.e., provincial grants), intentionally woo students who would ordinarily attend public schools.
7. Funding for education generally is becoming more and more a concern for government, with some critics forecasting great savings in the unification of all public education systems into one entity.
8. Many in the Catholic community and other faith communities believe that it is the fundamental right of parents to decide the type of education that is best for their children,

and believe that government has the responsibility to provide such education.

9. The constitutional right for Catholic education is very clear.
10. The United Nations Commission on Human Rights has ruled that the Ontario government is out of line in funding one faith's schools but denying school funding to other faith communities.
11. Quebec and Newfoundland and Labrador gave up their constitutional right to public Catholic schools.
12. On the Newfoundland and Labrador front: With the demise of public Catholic education comes an enormous challenge for the church to provide a faith education to Catholic children in that province (financially and in terms of finding qualified personnel).
13. Other provinces (British Columbia, Alberta, Saskatchewan, Manitoba, Quebec) have public funding—complete or partial—for faith-based schools.
14. The bishops of Ontario support faith-based schools in their efforts for funding.
15. The Ontario English Catholic Teachers' Association (OECTA) has been opposed to public funding for faith-based schools.
16. The toil, hardship, suffering and sacrifice that went into the establishment and maintenance of Catholic education in Ontario on the part of generations of laity and religious and clergy remain a matter of historical record. (This might be an important moment to become reacquainted with Mark McGowan's *The Enduring Gift*—in video or text format—an invaluable, concise account of our Catholic education story.)
17. A significant minority making up the Catholic education community—teachers, administrators, trustees and parents—really do see their work as living out their baptismal

vocation and as engaging in furthering the mission of the church.

18. There is an unfortunate lack of awareness (maybe even a lack of valuing) of the Catholic education story on the part of too many parents and too many Catholic educators (including teachers, trustees and administrators).
19. Some priests are reticent about promoting Catholic education and Catholic schools. This lack of support and enthusiasm at the parish level is a psychological obstacle to the work that committed Catholic educators try to do in their schools.
20. There is a dearth of qualified religious educators and theologians now connected with Catholic education in Ontario. Theology is the fundamental resource for an effective operative vision, board direction, chaplaincy / pastoral ministry and religious education. There are too few theological resource persons in Ontario's Catholic education system.
21. The church and the Catholic education community are experiencing new energy and a more joyful, confident approach to living our faith and witnessing to Jesus as a result of the election of Pope Francis in 2013.
22. Catholic education continues to be an anomaly. It made sense for the Catholic minority in 1867; it made sense to "compromise" (the Protestant minority in Quebec and the Catholic minority in Ontario), but it makes no sense today for one faith to have publicly funded schools while this same privilege is denied to other faiths.
23. Recent court judgments have been settled in favour of parents who wish to withdraw their children from religion classes and of non-Catholic parents who do not want their children at liturgical services in school.

Examining the Shift

What has changed? Let me identify three fundamental movements that I believe constitute the foundation for the new playing field (the paradigm shift) in which the drama of Catholic education in Ontario is now unfolding.

Faith and Religion versus Secular Ideology

The tension existing between faith and secular ideology is global in scope. The extended debate around faith-based education in 2007 made it clear that Ontario is home to the same phenomenon experienced in many jurisdictions in the West and in the developing world. *Faith meets the modern world!* Faith must work at some sort of accommodation with modernity, and the modern (postmodern) world must deal with the reality of faith and religion—a reality that, in spite of modernity's secular theories and presumptions, simply will not die out or go away. For instance, in many countries where Islam is the dominant faith, problems surround the modern innovations and lifestyle options from the West. Meanwhile, in France, a very secular state, there are problems because of the ban on covering one's face in public with a veil, such as a hijab, and because some religious minorities do not give in easily or accommodate to the ways of a secular state. (Indeed, we need only go next door to Quebec and its discussion around a charter of secular values.) Since the French Revolution, France has been fiercely proud and protective of its *laïcité* (secular-ness). With heavy immigration from Islamic countries, many in France now feel that their secular option is under attack.

Clearly, in Ontario, in a more muted way, something similar is taking place: we have the faith / religion versus secular ideology battleground. Some believe that faith / religion should be lived out in every aspect of life. An important dimension of this mindset is to do education in a faith environment and in a faith community, as the Catholic education community does. Others feel that religion is a completely private option that should have no privilege when it comes to public funds. Some "intellectuals" feel that Catholic education will be phased out eventually. Their view: the Catholic system exists, but it would be better if it did not exist, that it did not receive public funds. Basically, their position is that publicly funded Catholic education makes no sense at all in a modern (postmodern) secular society. From what goes on elsewhere in the world, one can safely bet that this tension will only increase here in Ontario, and that it will continue to impact publicly funded Catholic education. Ontario is becoming increasingly protective of its secular-ness. How is the Catholic education community preparing to dialogue with the proponents of the secular option that privatizes faith and religion and that deprives them of any subsidy from the public purse?

A More Coherent Articulation for Social Cohesion

A more forceful and coherent articulation states that what was acceptable at the time of Confederation is no longer good for Ontario in 2014. Yakabuski insists that a constitutional right in 1867 that made Canada possible is now seen to be an obstacle to unity. In this argument, social cohesion becomes the great urgency for the body politic of Ontario, and public education is the last standing agent to affect social cohesion, given that so many social institutions (family, church and religion) are now fragmented or greatly diminished. There is much more diversity in the Ontario of today than there was in 1867. The Canadian bishops, in their December 2013 *Essential Elements* document, underscore pluralism as the fundamental context for evangelization today. This diversity is not just present through more Christian churches; it is made up of Jews, Muslims, Hindus, Buddhists, Sikhs, and those of other faiths, along with articulate secularists. As well, due to the strong anti-Catholic education and anti–faith-based education lobbies, more and more folks are now aware that Newfoundland and Labrador and Quebec gave up their constitutional rights regarding education. And this can happen in Ontario as well.

The great challenge for Catholic education is to demonstrate to the Ontario public that Catholic education makes a difference: that the common project of Ontario society would be diminished without Catholic schools. The public must also be educated on the particular reasons for Newfoundland and Labrador giving up its constitutional right to Catholic schools and for Quebec's decision to give up its right to Catholic schools. The media present misleading oversimplifications that must be challenged. The conditions in Ontario are very different from the contexts in Quebec and Newfoundland and Labrador. How prepared is the Catholic education community to demonstrate that the social fabric and common life of Ontario would be diminished without a publicly financed Catholic education system?

Catholic Education and the Question of Catholic Identity

It is not surprising that increased secularization brings with it new challenges to maintaining the Catholic identity of our schools and, indeed, the Catholic identity of the entire Catholic education experience in Ontario. "How Catholic is Catholic?" is the new question. Or "How much Catholic is necessary to preserve the integrity of our Catholic education?"

On the one hand, there is an urgent need to emphasize Catholic identity in order to be faithful to our original purpose and founding mission. So *traditio fidei*, the handing down of our faith—evangelization, knowing the Catholic Christian story, understanding and promoting our tradition and our vision for Catholic education—is deemed essential to maintaining the integrity of Catholic education and to effectively continuing our mission. This is what one might call capital-C Catholic education! I feel that this capital-C Catholic education is what fuels the approach of a significant minority of the partners in Catholic education—teachers, parents, administrators and trustees. They have a strong sense of vocation, of living out their Baptism; they sense that what they are about in the Catholic school really is to participate in the mission of the church.

On the other hand, there is Catholic education described as small-c catholic—"Here comes everyone!" As I have observed often in this journal, many of the children now in our Catholic schools come from Catholic families that do not seem to place a high priority on participating regularly in their parish, and especially at Sunday Eucharist. I suspect that this is also the case for more than a few Catholic teachers and administrators. This is not to be critical. It is simply a sociological observation, putting in writing what is happening. These Catholics have been called "occasional Catholics"—a happier descriptive, surely, than "unchurched" or even "non-practising." Participating in the Sunday Eucharist on a regular basis is the hallmark of living our Catholic faith. (There are other ways of living and practising one's faith as well, of course. I do not want to limit this "How Catholic is Catholic?" question to the pastoral reference or to regular Sunday Mass attendance. My great hope and wish is that each Catholic would own his or her baptismal priesthood and would continue to develop in their faith in Jesus and as members of the church.) The point to make here is that for these parents, teachers and administrators, Catholic identity does not seem to be strong; they only faintly appreciate the Catholic Christian story. The force of the secularizing process has whittled away at the possibility of a convinced ownership of one's baptismal priesthood and Catholic faith. And if that ownership is absent from the mind and the heart, it is certainly not going to be felt in the practice of Catholic education.

Evidence of this compromised or watered-down Catholic identity can be detected in conversations with teachers that take place around the pastoral reference. Evidence, too, is gleaned from working with teachers, presuming some elementary understanding of faith and discovering that it is just not there. (On the plus side, we are blessed that at least all of our teachers have had a fundamental formation experience in an obligatory religion course that is a prerequisite for hiring. While this is something, the challenge of these times demands deeper, ongoing formation experiences.) In regards to parents, evidence is gleaned from the conversations and discussions that take place in meetings with those in preparation for the sacraments of Baptism, Confirmation and First Eucharist. An indicator of secularization is a conversation with a couple looking to baptize their child: "But Father, none of our friends really practise their faith. It is so hard to find Catholics serious about their faith to be godparents or Confirmation sponsors!"

Now here, for me, is the rub! I believe that a strong sense of Catholic identity—capital-C Catholic identity—is a must if we are not only to preserve Catholic education but add to the tradition of Catholic education as well. The lived Catholicism of each generation has within it insights and understandings that enrich the Catholic education experience from one generation to the next.

Back to the question "How much Catholic is necessary to preserve the integrity of Catholic education?" The case might be made that the quality of the Catholic education offered now in our boards and schools is largely determined by the active, committed presence of those partners in Catholic education who are capital-C Catholic. These are the women and men who see their participation in the Catholic education project and in their teaching as living out their Baptism vocation and who understand the Catholic school as being vital dimensions of the mission of the church. The case might also be made now that, among the Catholic education partners, the small-c catholic representation is increasing, and the capital-C Catholic representation is decreasing. This is worrisome. If it comes to the crunch, I don't think we can expect much intelligent strategy or passion or energy from small-c catholics to speak for Catholic education and act for Catholic education. *Nemo dat quod non habet!* One can't give what one does not have.

Catholic identity is also under siege by the increasing number of non-Catholic Christians and secularists who choose our schools for reasons such as proximity, sports, academics, test scores, discipline, the possibility of talking about God and prayer, etc. Several secular commentators, along with increased numbers of non-Catholics and even non-Christians, refer to the small-c catholic reality and conclude that as the years go by, the secularization process gradually but inevitably is eroding Catholic identity and thereby diminishing the distinctive difference between public education and public Catholic education. They see Catholic schools as being well along the path of secularization—which means that soon Catholic schools will be so secularized, there will be very little difference between a Catholic school and a public school.

Conclusion

It is now 30 years since full funding of Catholic education began. For most of that time, Catholic education has expanded in every part of Ontario. With the new-found financial security, along with the growth in schools and numbers of students and teachers, a mindset of entitlement may have developed: "We have a right to this system." With such a mindset, the sacrifice and struggles of the past are easily forgotten, and a relevant working vision for Catholic education owned by Catholic educators is simply taken for granted. Questions about what struggle and sacrifice may be required today remain unasked.

Because of the new secularizing situation for publicly funded Catholic education in this province, the mindset of entitlement must give way to some profound soul-searching. Contemporary Ontario culture is increasingly suspicious of the privilege that any religious group might enjoy when it comes to public funds. In our society today, there is a more coherent understanding of diversity in the province and of the exigency to have all students belong to the same school system—one public system—for the purposes of socialization into civic life. Within the Catholic community, the question of "How Catholic is Catholic?" as it relates to our Catholic school system begs to be addressed. Can small-c catholic survive for long on its own without being renewed in the large-C Catholic identity?

For the last quarter century, a number of Catholic education documents and vision statements have attempted to define ourselves in Catholic education. (The ownership of and commitment to these often articulate, inspiring, challenging documents and vision statements is another question.) The point is that there have been few outside pressures or challenges to the specific Catholic nature of our system. But now there are other forces defining who we are: proponents of a secularizing culture who hold that in ten years' time, there will be little difference between a public system and a small-c catholic system; a political and civil rights lobby that sees a separate Catholic system as an obstacle to the common good of Ontario society; constituencies both inside and outside the Catholic school community that raise uneasy questions about what the Catholic difference really is and whether it is significant enough to justify two systems.

Since full funding in 1984, Ontario culture clearly has become more secular; personal and family identity with faith traditions and religious institutions have noticeably diminished. This makes a serious study of the Catholic identity question by all the partners and in every school a crucial exercise to the present and future of publicly funded Catholic education in this province.

We must get on with searching for the soul of Catholic education. Now!

REFLECTION 2

The New Evangelization for Parish and School: The Moment for Renewed Collaboration

I see this reflection as presenting both challenge and gift. The challenge is for parishes and Catholic schools to intentionally increase their collaboration for the sake of the gospel. The gift is in the joy and excitement when positive collaboration is realized.

One sometimes speaks of crisis as a time for fear and uncertainty. One can also speak of crisis as *kairos* time, an opening time, a privileged opportunity to really work at one's purpose or project in a fresh and imaginative way. I think we should look at the present "crisis" regarding evangelizing in Canada today as a *kairos* moment, an opportunity to take full advantage of the richness of our Catholic schools. I see this advantage at work in the relationship between parish and school. I am aware that some people, including some priests, wonder about the orthodoxy and sincerity of Catholic schools and Catholic teachers. No doubt, in a few instances this wondering is justified. But for the great number of Catholic schools and Catholic educators, I firmly believe that we must assume goodwill, the best of intentions and some very effective evangelizing. In this reflection, I want to address this tension that may exist between parish and school and to propose the ideal of collaborative ministry as an example of evangelizing outreach.

I am writing this reflection in March 2014. For a year now, Pope Francis has been the bishop of Rome. On numerous occasions over the last twelve months, the Holy Father has stated that the church is a church for everyone. It is an inclusive church, not an exclusive church. It is a welcoming, hospitable community, not a community closed in on itself. In a word, the church is a church for the many, not for the few.

Pope Francis' inclusivity resonates with the practical theology I absorbed some 40 years ago. In 1975, I was studying at the Institut catholique in Paris. Several times that year, I would take a weekend and journey by train a couple of hours southwest of Paris to Le Mans. Le Mans is the birthplace of my religious community, the Congregation of Holy Cross. Our mother foundation is situated in Le Mans, and my good friend and classmate Louis was, at the time, the pastor of the mother church. Studying in France and observing the French ecclesial reality at a time when so few Catholics attended Mass on Sunday, perhaps 10 percent of the baptized, I would engage Louis with questions: "Why so few? Wouldn't it be better to not baptize the 90 percent unless there is a clear option to take the practice of their faith to heart?"

That year, I was taking a liturgy course with the renowned Jesuit Father Joseph Gelineau. In one lecture, he observed that the percentage of practising Catholics at the time of the French Revolution (1789) was no higher than in 1975. Father Gelineau and my friend Louis insisted that we must be open and welcoming when people come for Baptism, that somehow there must be grace at play, that the Holy Spirit must be present in most such requests. They both asked, "Who are we to judge?" God works in ways that are foreign to our thinking. I think their pastoral experience was at work as well—their experience with some who, while not regularly at Sunday Mass, were certainly Catholic in the way they acted and prayed and served.

The Canadian bishops, in their December 2013 document *The Essential Elements of Evangelization Today,* outline the new territory we must travel in our evangelizing efforts. Pluralism now colours the evangelizing landscape, which means different ways and approaches, different mindsets and different priorities. Pluralism invites us to appreciate the presence of the other and, at the same time, the difference of the other. Recognizing the pluralistic makeup of the Catholic school, the different ways and different levels of intensity of being Catholic, becomes the challenge for parish and school in our time. It is this call to be inclusive and welcoming in this pluralistic culture that is the new context for our Catholic schools and for the relationship of the parish with the students, teachers and parents of the Catholic school. The Holy Spirit calls us to be in the middle of things, as things are not as we would like them to be.

In the evangelizing project, this is the time for renewed collaboration between parish and school. The school provides the parish with contacts and connections, with possibilities for outreach to parishioners who are not often at Sunday worship. The parish offers the Catholic school the deep spiritual resources of the sacramental life, the proclamation of the Word and the possibility to be renewed in the school's reason for being. This is *kairos* time; it is not time for protecting our turf.

Overcoming Mistrust

But it is not easy. In my own experience and in listening through the years to the experience of others, mainly teachers and principals, I have found that, in a few instances, some clergy and some parishes are suspicious about the Catholic identity of the Catholic school. A split, almost a territorial division, exists between the parish and the school. Such a split is counterproductive to the evangelization that is called for today. We need to enlarge our notion of parish community and parish ministry. Because I emphasize the importance of parish and Catholic school collaborating for the sake of the gospel and handing on our faith to the children, and because my present ministry is situated in the parish, I work mainly from the questions and suspicions the parish priest may have concerning the Catholic school. But I am mindful that there is a flip side to this equation. Here I revert to my former ministry as Catholic educator and my experience with more than a few principals. There are cases where the principal representing the Catholic school has very little understanding of the centrality of parish in the life of the church, and feels no need to cooperate with the priest and the parish. My focus here, however, is more on priest and parish.

In my January 21 journal item on the phone call with a father who was seeking Baptism for his three children, I referred to the priest who, according to my caller, had very little confidence that the school was able to teach our Catholic tradition and hand on our faith. I don't believe that this is an isolated sentiment. I sense that clergy who insist that all sacramental preparation be done in the parish without any cooperation from the teachers in the school can be another expression of this lack of clerical confidence in the Catholic school. I am not sure what is at the bottom of this insistence: Does the priest know more than the teachers? Can the priest better monitor the orthodoxy of the catechetical formation taking place? Does the priest feel that, since the parish is where the sacraments are celebrated, it must also be the place where formation takes place? Is the church or parish seen as more sacred or holy than the school? Does the priest feel that the church is the parish and the school has no ecclesial standing? Does the priest / parish want to invite children and their parents to become comfortable in the parish and to realize that the parish church is their church?

The Primacy of Parish

Without a doubt, because of the Eucharist and the sacraments, the parish community has primacy. The parish is the focal point; Sunday Eucharist is celebrated in the parish church. The sacraments come from that celebration of the Eucharist and are celebrated in the parish church. Yet the evangelizing project is greater than the parish church. Evangelization happens outside the four walls of the church as well.

Let me refer here to the 1988 Vatican document I cite in the introduction to this book:

> The Catholic school finds its true justification in the mission of the Church; it is based on an educational philosophy in which faith, culture and life are brought into harmony. Through it the local Church evangelizes, educates and contributes to the formation of a healthy and morally sound life-style among its members. (*The Religious Dimension of Education in a Catholic School*, 34)

Two key pastoral points are emphasized here: the Catholic school is inherent to the mission of the Church, and the Catholic school has a relationship to the local church. (I interpret this as parish.)

Since 1989, when the pastoral letter on education, *This Moment of Promise,* was published, the Ontario bishops as a conference, and many bishops individually, have underscored the great good fortune we have in Ontario with a fully funded Catholic education system. The same good fortune applies to local churches in Alberta and Saskatchewan. I have been privileged to minister in a diocese in which the four bishops I have served have all given the greatest support to the ministry of the Catholic school and the work of Catholic educators.

But the Catholic school cannot define itself independently of the parish; it must be seen as working in harmony and in cooperation with the parish. Indeed, it must have a certain dependence on the parish: not in the sense of subservience, but on the spiritual leadership one has a right to expect from sacraments and spiritual life of the parish, from the parish and the parish priest.

The Challenge of Inclusiveness and Pluralism

At different points in this journal, I have claimed that, as church today, we need to go to where the people are, and not expect that the people will come to us, to the parish and the parish church. The old paradigm of parish and two or three priests, Masses and devotions going on all week, and great numbers of people coming to church no longer exists, or if it does exist, it is the exception. This is the new paradigm I have described in various ways throughout this journal: occasional Catholics; Catholic schools full of baptized children who have only a slight attachment to the local parish; some parents' difficulty in identifying people who would model the ideals one would like for a Catholic godparent or sponsor; some teachers who are small-c catholic when it comes to understanding and living out of their Baptism.

The foundation of the old paradigm is a Catholic culture that has broken down. The new paradigm, as Pope Francis and the Canadian bishops note, is the gospel imperative of inclusiveness, along with the challenge of pluralism. Pope Francis states, "We cannot passively and calmly wait in our church buildings; we need to move from a pastoral ministry of mere conservation to a decidedly missionary pastoral ministry" (*The Joy of the Gospel*, 15). An important aspect of the new evangelization is to help Catholics who are already baptized and admitted to Eucharist to recover their fervour and the meaning and beauty of their faith. This applies especially to so-called countries with a solid Christian history, such as Canada. As we have seen, the "Christian country" moniker no longer fits. Even though many Catholics, in Baptism and in name, have but a slight grasp of the meaning of our Catholic faith, their faith does mean something to them.

In January 2014, speaking to the leadership of a number of religious congregations, many of them ministering in Catholic education, Pope Francis remarked:

> The percentage of children studying in schools who have separated parents is very high. The situation in which we live now provides us with new challenges which sometimes are difficult to understand. How can we proclaim Christ to these boys and girls? How can we proclaim Christ to a generation that is changing? We must be careful not to administer a vaccine against faith to them.

This is another description of the new paradigm. In this new paradigm, the Catholic school can become a privileged place for "proclaiming Christ to a generation that is changing." Ministry directed to the Catholic school, to parents and staff and students, is taking the gospel to where the people are. Perhaps now the Catholic school is more important than ever in the evangelizing efforts of the church, both diocese and parish. By highlighting certain expectations—the parish's expectations of the Catholic school and the Catholic school's expectations of the parish—I think we can show how together school and parish can be an effective force for evangelizing in a pluralistic context.

What the Catholic School Needs from the Parish

One should never underestimate the power of encouragement. In the church and pastoral ministry, we often lament how complicated and difficult things are today. That same reality exists in teaching—and perhaps even more in administering a school. Teachers need encouragement and affirmation in their lay ministry. Twenty-five years ago, *This Moment of Promise* had it right about the vocation of the Catholic teacher:

> There is no doubt that it is you—teachers—who bear the heat of the day in Catholic education. The daily pressures you face are enormous and the rewards of teaching are sometimes long in coming. You deserve the support and understanding of all those involved in Catholic education. It is not necessary to be free of faults and failures to be faithful to the integrity of the process of Catholic education. Otherwise, none of us would dare be involved.

Teachers need encouragement; teachers deserve affirmation. This brief little paragraph should serve often as a meditation for anyone in the parish who does ministry and who collaborates with teachers in the school.

Catholic teachers are a great gift to the church in Ontario and, I would add, wherever we have Catholic schools in Canada. The gift comes in the exceptional quality of many women and men, through their natural gifts and energy. Added to this is the formation in the faith teachers have received through the religion courses they have taken. This formation and promotion of the laity is a Vatican II ideal. In Ontario alone, some 40,000 teachers have had a foundational introduction to the things of the faith. Of course one wishes that they had more biblical training, understanding of church teaching, ethical expertise and liturgical grounding. One wishes that there were fewer and fewer small-c catholics and more and more large-C Catholics. But every teacher in the Catholic school has some formation as a Catholic teacher. Teachers should be theologically aware enough to understand that theirs is a special vocation stemming from their Baptism. Teachers should know that the mission of the Catholic school is intimately tied into the mission of the church, which is to make Jesus known and loved, and to help children grow into their own gift of faith.

That initial formation as a Catholic teacher needs further formation. Formation is not a one-off. As in any profession, there is a need always to be updated and renewed. This is where the parish comes in. The parish and parish team have resources for this updating and renewal. A proclamation and preaching of the Word that inspires and challenges, along with meaningful liturgical celebration and worship are at the heart of such renewal. When well prepared and done with great heart, the celebration of the Eucharist for a group of students or a liturgical celebration for a class can be a moment of renewal for the Catholic educator as well.

A welcoming parish community becomes a model for the community of the Catholic school. The simple human gestures of kindness and hospitality tell so much about what this church community stands for. The Catholic school in the parish is usually pretty quick to adopt that same hospitable spirit for itself. The parish, through the priest and members of the pastoral team, can put feet on parish hospitality by frequent presence in the school. To have a coffee in the staff room, a chat in the corridor, a pop-in to the classroom or a walk about in the yard become strong affirmations that, yes, the parish community is very much united with you in your Catholic education ministry, and, yes, we value the evangelization outreach of this Catholic school community.

The Catholic school should be able to look to the theological resources of the parish for guidance and direction on some of the pressing social and ethical questions that define our times and shape how we live together. Increasingly, for example, euthanasia is becoming more acceptable and even natural to the Canadian imagination. Euthanasia is a scary prospect. In Belgium, euthanasia is now extended to children. Talk about a slippery slope. This is a question to be looked at critically in the Catholic school classroom through the lens of Catholic teaching on the sacredness of all life. In cases like this, the priest and the parish team can be very supportive to the evangelizing effort of the school by identifying the questions and providing resources to deal with them. The school becomes an extension of the parish.

And there is the church's preferential option for the poor. Here, too, the priest and parish can assist the Catholic school. The reality of poverty in Canada, the increasing gap between the rich and poor and the demand from different quarters for a living wage are examples of economic and social questions that should be studied within the framework of Catholic social teaching. And there are, of course, other contemporary questions demanding a faith response. These are the questions the priest and parish team could suggest to the teachers, along with recommending the appropriate resources for study. Together, the parish and the school can be an effective force for evangelization in a pluralistic context.

And finally, here is a very practical point. In conversations with principals and teachers, I am reminded that it is often through the children that one can reach the parents. The Catholic school is a privileged place for the priest and those on the pastoral team to connect with parents. This connection happens when priest and members of the parish are present to the children. The Catholic school is located in the parish; presumably, the parents of the Catholic children in the school are members of the parish. The reality is that many of these families do not have a strong attachment to the parish, aside from the Catholic school. Yet the challenge for the church today is to go out to meet people where they are. Pope Francis explains:

> The new evangelization is a summons … to the baptized whose lives do not reflect the demands of baptism, who lack a meaningful relationship to the Church and no longer experience the consolation born of faith. The Church in her maternal concern tries to help them experience a conversion which will restore the joy of faith to their hearts and inspire commitment to the Gospel. (*The Joy of the Gospel,* 14)

In this time of the new evangelization, the Catholic school that is serious about educating the children in faith and reaching the parents needs the positive collaboration of priest and parish. In turn, the priest and parish, in dialogue with the school, need to look for imaginative ways of being more present to the parents of Catholic school students.

What the Parish Needs from the Catholic School

According to canon law (Canon 777), the pastor is to make particular provision that suitable catechesis is given for the celebration of the sacraments, that children are properly prepared for reception of the sacraments, and that children are catechized more deeply after reception of the sacraments. Ours is not the largest of parishes, but it is large—there are about 1,100 children in our three elementary schools and 1,300 students in the Catholic high school. Throughout this journal and in these reflections, I point out the key role played by the Catholic school in educating the children in the faith. I began the journal by outlining the contents of our famous *Green Binder*, which highlights the collaboration of parish and school in the evangelizing project. In a word, the Catholic school is critically important in assisting the pastor and the parish in fulfilling its sacred mandate. This educating in the faith is what the parish needs above all from the Catholic school.

In a particular way in the parish, we are most appreciative of the teachers who help prepare the children for the sacraments. I have been fortunate to collaborate with some excellent faith educators who see their teaching as a ministry. Although a few others have disappointed, let me celebrate those who do a wonderful job. While we have been working hard with the invitation to parents to assume their fundamental role as first faith educators of their children, we continue to depend on the Catholic teacher as backup. On paper, it is ideal: the parent prepares the child for First Eucharist and Reconciliation and Confirmation. In reality, the response is uneven. Some parents just are not able to take on this role. The Catholic teacher is there to shower attention on all students, and maybe spend more time with the ones who will not get much catechesis at home. Such teachers become architects of the Catholic imagination, equipping children with a faith anchor to hold on to in the years to come.

For its part, the parish would welcome the pleasure of *your* presence more than anything else—the presence of the parents and especially of Catholic teachers and principals—at Sunday Eucharist. Wisdom handed down through the ages is part of the Christian community's vast treasure trove. The parish is a particular geographical expression that operates as the Christian community. As such, the parish can access wisdom. The gift of wisdom tells us that Sunday Sabbath is good and important for the baptized. It is good to hear God's Word; it is good to be nourished at the table of the Eucharist; it is good to stand in worship and praise Sunday after Sunday in the unity of faith with other members of the Christian community. As an extension of the parish, the school evangelizes, but the school itself is always in need of evangelization. The teachers as the adult animators of the Catholic school need their souls educated. To be faithful to their shared evangelizing project in this new paradigm, the priest and the parish would greatly value the teachers' presence and participation at Sunday Eucharist. The priest and the parish would love that each and every teacher live out with authenticity the ideals of the pastoral reference they have received.

Whether the Catholic school is physically adjacent to the church or 2 or 3 kilometres down the road, shared evangelization and shared ministry are the ideal. Teachers make an important contribution to parish liturgical life when they volunteer as readers and ministers of communion. Parish committees and services are enriched by the presence of teachers. There is the power of witness at play as well. In a sense, the Catholic teacher is a public person often known by many parishioners. While the teacher does not come to Mass to be seen, the teacher *is* seen. And her presence or his participation does have an impact. Some parishioners comment, "It is uplifting to see teachers live their faith." Folks know that this lived faith will be felt in the classroom, in relationship with students. It gives further validation to Catholic education participating in the mission of the church.

In the previous reflection, I examined the urgency that publicly funded Catholic education faces in expressing why it is still needed in a dramatically changing political and social context. Sustaining Catholic identity in a pluralistic culture and in an increasingly secular society is an enormous challenge for Catholic education and the Catholic school. So if that is the challenge, let me ask this question: "Who is responsible for taking up the challenge to protect and foster Catholic identity?" The safe answer would be all of the partners of Catholic education: parents, the diocese and parishes, trustees, administrative officers, principals and teachers. Safeguarding Catholic identity rests in the hands and hearts of all who care for Catholic education. From our vantage point in the parish, we see this as almost a sacred responsibility of each teacher in the Catholic school. But because there is so much at stake in maintaining the Catholic identity of the school, the priest and the parish also have a sacred responsibility to be supportive. It is the priest who rubs shoulders with the principal and the staff. It is to the priest that the school often looks for answers when it comes to faith questions and church issues. It is the priest who animates the school liturgies during the year. It is the preaching and teaching of the priest that can identify for the school community reasons to be thankful and areas of concern. In all of this, the priest and parish can serve as a conscience, a determined but gentle voice, urging the Catholic school community to continually be aware of maintaining the Catholic character of the school. I emphasize conscience as a determined but gentle voice. This type of voice can be a gift to the school, and it extends the invitation to the school to collaborate with the parish in the evangelizing project with the parents and their children.

Conclusion

In the last few years, the church has claimed the need for a new evangelization. In my mind, the classic understanding of evangelization in our times is found in Pope Paul VI's 1976 apostolic exhortation, *On Evangelization in the Modern World* (*Evangelii Nuntiandi*). So many recent church documents continue to refer to this practical yet significant theology. But now we are rightly focusing on the "new" aspect of evangelization. Since 1976 in the Canadian church, I see something new in the pastoral attention and outreach we are invited to extend to those who are Catholics in name and by Baptism, but who do not participate regularly in the sacramental life of the church and who need encouragement and invitation to help them recover the fervour of their Baptism. As we have seen, many of the families in our Catholic schools would be included here. Also, since 1976, I see many new aspects in the context in which we find ourselves trying to live our faith and pass on our faith to our children. This is the heavily secular and pluralistic culture that is Canadian society. Pope Francis helpfully invites us to see ourselves as missionaries and to see one common evangelizing project in the mission of the parish and of the Catholic school. The families in the Catholic school are families belonging to the parish. Both school and parish are called to proclaim the gospel of Jesus by witness and word and to invite these families to recover the experience of how much God loves us in the gift of the Eucharist—or even to realize this for the first time. The more we can minister together, collaborating in our service and witness and teaching, the more faithful we will be to our vocation to evangelize, and to evangelize in a new way. Pope Francis states:

> Pastoral ministry in a missionary key seeks to abandon the complacent attitude that says: We have always done it this way. I invite everyone to be bold and creative in this task of rethinking the goals, structures, style and methods of evangelization in their respective communities. (*The Joy of the Gospel*, 330)

As for success, that really is the Lord's call. Our call is to be creative … to be faithful … to keep at it.

REFLECTION 3

Elements of a Spirituality for the Catholic Educator

Throughout this journal, two persistent themes contribute to shaping the contemporary Catholic education project: the very perplexing nature of secular culture, and the insistence that doing Catholic education is a vocation. The church in its expression as parish has lofty expectations of those who do Catholic education—teachers and principals primarily, but also trustees, board administrators and parents who take seriously their role as Catholic parents. Over these months, I have been journalling as a pastor. I have referred to the beguiling nature of the culture, and I have underscored that teaching in the Catholic school is a vocation. In my reflection on the parish and school, I observed that the school, the principal and staff, have a right to expect spiritual nourishment and encouragement from the priest and the parish. Those who are engaged in educating the soul have a right to have their own souls nourished as well. A practical spirituality is very helpful for keeping alive one's interior life—one's life of the soul. It is as a pastor that I offer this meditation on spirituality, and I do so hoping that some will find sustenance in it for their own souls.

Spirituality can mean many things to many different people. For me, it means tending to the things of the spirit or caring for the health of one's interior life. I would like to focus on some building blocks for a spirituality for Catholic educators, and by this I mean all of the partners of Catholic education. This is a very personal reflection in that I depend for the most part on examining and sharing my own practice and my own experience. I feel that the best thing I can offer, and that which I feel most comfortable offering, is what works for me: what keeps me going, what allows me to keep coping, to keep in the struggle. My purpose is to share a model of what a lived spirituality might look like. The richest part of one's spirituality is surely one's own experience. It is in one's life—one's experience—that God is active and that God reveals himself. Perhaps one of the great spiritual problems of our time is that we are not used to reflecting on and discerning that personal experience in which God is so active and reveals himself.

Back in my classroom days, my friend used to tease me that he had 25 years' experience in teaching while I had only 18 years. But I would say: "No! You have it all wrong. You have one year of experience repeated 25 times!" He was not someone given to much thinking or reflecting about what he was about or what he was doing … or why. To get serious about spirituality is to get serious about owning and deepening one's own experience: as a person in relationship with loved ones and significant others, as a believer in Jesus, and as one called to serve the project of Catholic education.

"Come no closer. Remove the sandals from your feet, for the place on which you are standing is holy ground." (Exodus 3:1-6) This is the Lord speaking to Moses from the burning bush. The place on which we stand is always our own history, our own blessings and burdens, our own experience. It is that *life experience* and that *experience of life* that we must reverence, pay attention to and learn from. That is our holy ground. It is especially here that the Holy Spirit speaks to us. I would like to humbly propose and comment on five elements that I believe can serve as a healthy and helpful framework for a working spirituality for all those involved in Catholic education. It works for me. I hope it will work for you!

1. Gratitude

Many years ago, when I was beginning to learn about prayer and the spiritual life, I was taught the acronym ACTS—Adoration, Contrition, Thanksgiving, Supplication. These are the four types of prayer. By far, the easiest form of prayer for me is *thanksgiving.* Gratitude. *The place on which you stand is holy ground*—that is my experience. And my experience is always contextualized. I have a beginning, a genesis, roots. What I am—who I am—I owe to many others who have helped shape me and form me. How easy prayer of gratitude is when I put it this way. How meaningful and purposeful life becomes when I can simply call on God to bless those who give such precious value to my life. This prayer of blessing soon becomes a litany of gratitude.

One of the great surprises for me is that most teachers, most of the time, find immense satisfaction in what they are about in the classroom. *How do you like your class this year? I absolutely love it. These are the greatest kids.* I say it is a surprise because we too often hear how hard it is to teach these days, that the kids are so difficult. Liking one's students and enjoying teaching are both profound reasons simply to be grateful and to be so intentionally and often in prayer. As a pastor prays daily for people of the parish, so should it be natural for the teacher to pray daily for the students in her care and to single out in prayer the kids who may be struggling. The classroom or the administrator's office is especially holy ground for the Catholic educator.

To take for granted is the thief that robs us of the ability and capacity to give thanks. This is so easy to do when one leads an unreflected life. Mary Jo Leddy writes of the culture of dissatisfaction (*Radical Gratitude*, Orbis, 2002). Our culture of dissatisfaction is not gratitude friendly. When I say "thank you," what is implied is that I have enough or more than enough. But the culture of dissatisfaction (we are never satisfied) refuses to recognize *enough*—there always has to be more; we quickly move from satisfaction to dissatisfaction. I am not enough; I do not have enough. And we get so sucked into believing that we really are incomplete and that we really don't have enough. The culture of private property also dictates against a spirit that is open and dependent on God's gracious goodness. Private property says, "This is mine. It is the work of my hands. I am responsible for my success. It has been my inventiveness and my hard work and my saving and my investing." We are shaped from our earliest days to think like this. It is a cultural hazard. But the first victim of this type of thinking is God and God's gracious goodness to me. Surely what I am and what I have ultimately are gifts from God. Surely my talents and skills and brains are gifts from God. Surely my context and place in life are part of God's plan for me. Surely my health and energy and personality are all from God. And they are intended by God to serve him and to praise him and to love him.

Many poor countries don't have a Thanksgiving Day. It is a good thing that we have a Thanksgiving Day, a time to pause and to appreciate the people and things that make our life so rich. Yet it is too easy to become complacent and to think *Yes! This is God's established order. This is the way things should be.* There should be a strong streak of dissatisfaction or an uneasy tension in our Thanksgiving Days. We are blessed indeed, but we don't own these things; they are not ours. They are given to us to use and to share. St. Basil, a father of the early church, put it this way:

> The bread in your cupboard belongs to the hungry; the coat hanging unused in your closet belongs to the one who needs it; the shoes rotting in your closet belong to the one who has no shoes; the money you put in the bank belongs to the poor. You do wrong to everyone you could help, but fail to help.

For me, any reflection on gratitude or on thanksgiving necessarily leads me to the great act of thanksgiving in my life, which is the celebration of the Eucharist. The Eucharist is the centre of my life as a Christian and my life as a priest. On Sunday, the day of the Lord, believers in Jesus gather to hear the Word of God in the proclamation of the scriptures. God's Word always nourishes and consoles; it challenges and gives direction to life. And the celebration at the table is the occasion to remember that Jesus took the sins of all time and the sins of all people with him on the cross, and in dying gave us salvation and eternal life. *Do this in memory of me!* Jesus not only left for us his body and blood to strengthen us—to make us one—but in eating and drinking of his body and blood, we become the Body of Christ to continue his presence and work in our world. *Go and announce the gospel of the Lord!*

The deeper we get into gratitude, the more powerful it becomes for us as the fundamental context and attitude for living. Here we begin to appreciate that even our crosses, our suffering, our setbacks can be stuff to give thanks for. This usually comes well after the fact when, in retrospect, we realize that God's plan for us was much different than we had imagined. This deviation or disappointment, while painful at the time, actually has opened up new possibilities for me. And gratitude, the attitude of gratitude, is essential as a starting point for real sorrow. *To the one who has been given much, much will be expected!* When I have this openness to see how much I depend on God and God's gracious gifts in my life, then I can more fully appreciate my sin. The more thanksgiving is a part of my life, the quicker I am able to identify my selfishness or sin. This is not a matter of feeling guilty. It is, rather, a very realistic way of seeing that I have taken advantage of God who has so richly blessed me in life. It is in getting in touch with those many blessings that allows me to feel my sin and seek pardon.

The prayer of thanksgiving, saying, "Thank you, Lord" often, is the easiest and most natural starting point in considering a practical spirituality for all involved in the Catholic education project.

2. Vocation or Call

The idea or notion of call is fundamental to my spirituality. My stance before God is a stance of relationship. God is a person. God is a person who has called and chosen me. God is the ground of my being. The gift of faith in God is central to who I am, to my definition of self. This does not mean that faith is easy, a piece of cake. Faith can be difficult and challenging. Faith is hoping, but not always knowing. There are doubts to faith; there is uncertainty. Indeed, in a way, the more one knows about theology and the way the institutional church functions, the harder faith can be. *Where is the Holy Spirit here? What if it all is for nothing? Suppose that it is all myth! And at that hour of my death—the fear!*

But at the same time, faith is the profoundly rich substratum to my life. My faith in Jesus means that I am in an ongoing conversation with him. The image of vine and branches—Jesus is the vine and I am one of the branches—is the defining biblical image in my life. Without Jesus, I can do nothing. Attached to Jesus, I am to bear much fruit. Faith makes possible a happy, joyful, hopeful spirit; faith allows me to see God in all things, events and people. Faith permits me to experience the finger of God working in my life and in the world. In faith I experience call, a call by name, a call of a God who holds me in the palm of his hands, a call to be someone who I am not always ready to become, or to do something that I would sooner not do. The call is always there. It's not as if there was a call at one moment, and then the line went dead. It is a call that comes through the everyday stuff of my life, of my experience. This call begs for a daily listening response.

One of the great riches of the Second Vatican Council was the reawakening of the church to the fundamental vocation of Baptism: the idea that vocation comes with what it is to be a Christian. For too long, vocation was limited to priesthood and religious life. In a way, the baptismal vocation relativized the vocation to priesthood and religious life. But that is all right. Indeed, that is good. What really counts is the call, the vocation, that comes with Baptism. The reawakening of the vocation at Baptism includes the notion that ministry or service is part of living Baptism. Each of us is anointed *priest, prophet and king.* We now have our particular role to play in implementing Jesus' great gospel project. Pope Francis puts it this way:

> The new evangelization calls for personal involvement on the part of each of the baptized. Every Christian is challenged,

> here and now, to be actively engaged in evangelization; indeed, anyone who has truly experienced God's saving love does not need much time or lengthy training to go out and proclaim that love. Every Christian is a missionary to the extent that he or she has encountered the love of God in Christ Jesus: we no longer say that we are "disciples" and 'missionaries", but rather that we are always *missionary disciples*. (*The Joy of the Gospel*, 120)

How natural it is to see the vocation of Catholic educator as giving further shape to one's baptismal priesthood. And how rich it is for that person whose service is to the Catholic education project.

We can look at this even more fundamentally. Every person who lives has a call, a purpose for existence. Every person living has a special task, a purpose to accomplish for God. John Henry Newman, speaking about vocation, said, "God has created me to do him some definite service. He has committed work to me, which he has not committed to another. I have my mission—I may never know it in this life, but I shall be told it in the next." This gets us into mystery. What is the role of the infant who is born with severe disabilities? What is the purpose of the elderly beggar woman in rags who must live on scraps of garbage? We may never know it in this life, but we will be told it in the next.

It was only in my last years as a teacher that I succeeded in getting a little insight into the absolute importance of vocation and working with students to help them catch on to their own call from God. And yet, it seems to me now, this is something we have to begin working at from the very beginning, in kindergarten, in our prayers, in our conversations and in our teaching with our students. In a sense, there is nothing more important for us to do in Catholic education than to insist on vocation and call. I observed this in the journal item on Lenten Confessions and the Trinitarian prayer. Education is for life. For us as believers, what could be more important in the whole of life than our relationship with our Lord and Creator, the one who called us into being and continues to do so? The Catholic educator, sensitive and working on his own vocation, is going to be very conscious of awakening the reality of vocation in each of his students.

My spirituality is shaped and energized and continues to be driven by my call, my vocation. This means being alert to the questions that are the stuff of life and of everyday living: "What are you calling me to today, Lord? Where are you calling me?" We can't get any more spiritual or any more serious about spirituality than when we are trying to discern God's call in life. To be conscious of our vocation is not an option for the Catholic educator. It must be an essential attitude.

3. Working at Interiority

I don't think that one can have a spirituality if one does not have a sense of one's inner self. In his prayer for the Christians in Ephesus, St. Paul says: "In the abundance of the Father's glory … may he … through his Spirit … enable you to grow in power with regard to your inner self … so that Christ may live in your hearts through faith" (Eph. 3:16-17). The inner self is where we are most at home with ourselves; it is me at my most authentic, my most fundamental, the core of my being. There has to be a whole life lived in the inner self. In Psalm 51, the psalmist refers to the inner self as "the inward being" and "the secret heart." This does not mean that we have dual personalities or a split life—an outer self and an inner self. What it means is that we go deeper into the one self that we are, and it is here in the inner self that we are most ourselves.

The inner self is a place where we must go to often. Pope Francis says:

> Spirit-filled evangelizers are evangelizers who pray and work. What is needed is the ability to cultivate an interior space, which can give a Christian meaning to commitment and activity. Without prolonged moments of adoration, of prayerful encounter with the word, of sincere conversation with the Lord, our work easily becomes meaningless; we lose energy as a result of weariness and difficulties and our fervor dies out. (*The Joy of the Gospel*, 262)

To give meaning and purpose to life, the inner self serves at the same time as the pilot's cockpit that governs direction and control, and the engine room that generates positive energy and action. The more we can live from the inner self, the more authentic life will be and the happier and more content we will be. So much of the culture today commands that we live on the surface; that it is appearance that counts; that we have to be doing and going at all times "madly off in all directions"; that we must be blanketed in noise. I love the T.S. Eliot line that describes the impact of the culture: "Distracted from distraction by distractions / Filled with fancies and empty of meaning / Tumid apathy with no concentration" ("Burnt Norton," III).

The culture today works overtime to see to the needs of and to feed the external self. Unfortunately, we experience spiritual famine when it comes to our inner selves. We are anemic; we are underdeveloped; we give neither the time nor the attention that the soul needs. Jesus said to his friends, the disciples, "'Come away to a lonely place all by yourselves and rest for a while,' for there were so many going and coming that they had no time even to eat. So they went off in a boat to a lonely place where they could be by themselves" (Mark 6:30-34). The lonely place—the deserted place—the desert—the wilderness—the mountaintop: these are the biblical terms for that *space* and *place* and necessary personal time alone that every disciple must have. Translated into our own personal geography, that desert place could be a kitchen table with a cup of coffee, where we quietly think and pray; it could be a chair in the backyard where we sit alone; it could mean walking in the woods or driving in a car, alone, reflecting with a prayer in our hearts.

We all need the lonely place built into the daily routine of our lives, because it is at the lonely place that we can most easily access the inner self. The lonely place is only possible with quiet and silence. The question is "Where is my lonely place? How do I get to that lonely place?" At the level of my inner self, two things happen. First, I have an ongoing conversation with myself regarding vocation and call, sense of direction and purpose, quality of life lived and relationships experienced. In talking to myself, I really converse with my Lord, my Creator, the One who has called me into being. This is what we mean by *discernment*—trying to figure out God's will in my life; this discernment is an ongoing process, because God is always active and present in my life in so many different ways. The second thing that happens in my inner self is "that I just am." I pray; I contemplate. Again, T.S. Eliot refers to this place and space as "the still point": "At the still point of the turning world ... there the dance is" ("Burnt Norton," II). And ... "I said to my soul, be still, and let the dark come upon you / Which shall be the darkness of God" ("East Coker," III).

How hard it is for us to just sit and be in God's presence! To be at the still point. To let go of everything and just be in God's presence. It is so countercultural! So inefficient! So unproductive to simply sit for 10 minutes and realize that God loves us unconditionally and absolutely for who we are, not for what we do. And yet, it is this form of prayer that is so rich, so nourishing, so helpful for us to have perspective and an attitude for life and relationships. To do this frequently, daily for 10 minutes or so, to simply sit and be. This is the prayer that informs our practice, our life and activity.

Some of us must recover interiority, to take back the space and the place of the inner self. Some of us must discover interiority as for the first time. This is to grasp the fact that life is meant to be lived below the surface; that real meaning can be found only at the still point and in that very personal ongoing conversation between self and Creator-God. A spirituality without interiority is bubblegum spirituality, with no lasting value, and with no chance for us to become the person our Creator-God wants us to become.

It should be an imperative for us to form our students in interiority. In any vision of Catholic education, forming in prayer and introducing students to our Creator-God should be greatly privileged. The spiritual dimension of education must be central to all Catholic education. And how much more important and necessary this is today, given the fragility of most family life, which is the natural context for this formative experience.

Unless we are comfortable inhabiting and spending time in our own inner selves, it will be impossible to share this with our students. And if we haven't mastered this second language of conversation with God, which is prayer, our teaching as Catholic educators will be empty.

4. Forgiving and Being Forgiven

My experience is that forgiveness, both giving and asking, must be at the heart of spirituality. I have already mentioned that the person who has a refined sense of gratitude is also going to be able to easily recognize his or her own selfishness and sin. The more we have a sense of how God is good and gracious to us, the more we are going to feel sorrow for taking this goodness for granted and for breaking the bond of friendship with God. The more you love a person, the deeper the hurt when you betray or let down that person, and the more urgent the need for healing and reconciling.

The point of departure for my examination of conscience is this: God has been and continues to be so good to me—and this is my response: my pride / my egoism / my selfishness / my readiness to live life on the surface, avoiding the struggle and sidestepping the cross. It is in recognizing God's gracious gifts to me that I can more readily feel my sin and ask for forgiveness.

While deeply personal, our spirituality is also fundamentally social. We are always in relationship. We are, at times, hurt by others; we do, at times, hurt others. And so the ongoing reflex is to be able to forgive and to ask forgiveness. So much psychological and emotional pain exists in families today because of the inability to forgive; so much tension and conflict exist globally, in the community of nations, because of the inability to forgive. "Forgive us our trespasses as we forgive those who trespass against us." As this forgiveness and need to forgive are at the very heart of the prayer Jesus taught us, so they must be at the core of our spiritual life.

Again, our culture does not give us much help with the forgiveness element of spirituality. A culture that promotes being number one, rugged independence, getting even, and so on is not a culture that is conducive to forgiving and asking forgiveness. As Catholic educators, we must always have in mind that the culture is the fundamental, formative influence on our students. As we are so formidably challenged by the culture to help our kids develop a sense of interiority, the inner self, so we are challenged to form them in the art of healing and reconciling, and to give them the tools to repair the relational ruptures that lead to pain and hurt.

5. Exteriority—A Life Directed by Mission

The church has declared St. Thérèse of Lisieux the patron of mission and missionaries. Thérèse was a contemplative, a person with an intense spiritual life who never left the cloister and who died at a very young age. But she had constantly in her mind and in her heart the global needs and the global mission of the Kingdom. In that lonely place and space where we realize the inner self, we also bring our life and work. We bring our life and work for review, to mine our life and work for continued meaning, for understanding and perspective and future direction. There is a social dimension to spirituality; there has to be the social dimension, or our spirituality would be private! A privatized spirituality is simply an exercise in excessive individualism and feel-good self-development.

All Catholic educators, by the very nature of their vocation, are women and men on a mission. This mission and the needs and questions of the mission can be the content of the everyday prayer of Catholic educators. It is good to rise for a moment or so in your heart and mind above the nitty-gritty of daily routine, and to ask God's blessing on the common mission of handing on our faith in Jesus and teaching the things of the Kingdom of God.

An authentic spirituality also means trying to understand some of the structures that are obstacles to mission: economic poverty, the lack of social supports for poor families, the special needs of students, domestic violence, the everyday crosses and struggles of staff and students, the pressing ecological concerns. To be sure, it is a struggle, but because it is so attached to the mission of Catholic education, it is a holy struggle. As much as possible, prayer and analysis should lead to some kind of action.

Engagement in the struggle is the important thing. It could very well be that one won't see a lot of success, that achievements may be hard to find. We must get in the habit of letting the Holy Spirit see to our success. The critical thing is to carry on in the struggle. We can't confuse achievement and commitment; commitment to the mission is our task. Achievement in the mission is the Holy Spirit's worry. Bringing our work questions and our mission questions to prayer helps to make our prayer more focused and more urgent.

A further dimension of a healthy spirituality is the readiness to share with a group of colleagues who share our passion for the mission of Catholic education. For sure, it can be very lonely at times in the struggle. We need support; we need critique and input from others; we need to listen to different perspectives; we need to plan together and dream together about the mission of the Catholic school. There are times when it is very comforting to know that others are as confused and as fearful as we may be!

And that, too, can be helpful.

Conclusion

A good starting point in considering spirituality for all of the partners in Catholic education, including clergy, is to see how blessed we are to have fully funded Catholic education. We have so many possibilities for evangelizing through the instrument of Catholic education. We must never take for granted this enduring gift. The best source for acquiring a personal spirituality is to own one's experience and to reflect on that experience. It is in personal experience that God is most active and operative in life. It is in the act of reflection that, with God's grace, we can access what God says to us and where God is leading us. The act of reflection should be structured time and space; we need that personal lonely place. Many of us probably have tried allocating the time and the space. And for a while, we make a go of being quiet and listening to the Holy Spirit from the depths of our inner self. Sometimes it works. But then it seems that, too often, we draw blanks. And we say, "I start off well and then … same old, same old!" But if the truth be known, that is the natural pattern of the spiritual life. We have to keep coming back, and trying over and over and over. Remember—the important thing is the commitment, not the success.

Reflection 4

Fostering the Catholic Imagination in the Catholic School

For a long time, I have had this intuition that the Catholic school and teachers—especially in the early years—who have an appreciation of the Catholic imagination and what helps create the Catholic imagination can give a great gift to our students, a gift that for many of them will last a lifetime.

I am working on this reflection in early April. I have been reviewing some pages of this journal. The entries for February 3, St. Blaise Day and the blessing of throats, and Ash Wednesday jump out at me. I attribute this to the interesting way the children appreciated the candles and the ashes. I am also taken with the prayer tables and prayer corners in the classrooms—tangible aids for devotion. Coincidentally, the other day as I was watching a news feature on television, I learned that a university in the United States is offering a theology course dedicated to the music of Bruce Springsteen. Filed away in my clippings folder is a quotation by the Irish theologian and priest Enda McDonagh from *The Tablet*, the British Catholic weekly, on the occasion of the funeral of his friend Seamus Heaney, the poet and Nobel prize winner. Heaney was, above all, a poet of the Catholic imagination. Bruce Springsteen and Seamus Heaney! They were both formed in their childhood and youth into our Catholic faith. Such a formation, I believe, helped shape their imagination. Somehow, their formation stuck, and elements of their Catholicism have come out in song and poem. My hunch is that sacramental things such as candles and ashes and statues and incense, for example, can help create the Catholic imagination. And given the power of the secular culture considered in the journal and in the preceding reflections, I am convinced that fostering a Catholic imagination fits very well into the framework of the purpose of a Catholic education.

Let me explain. Catholics stress that God is immanent to created reality. Bread and wine and water and oil are sacramental signs of the encounter with the All Holy. For Catholics, it is through the concrete, the material, or through nature that we tend to experience the Divine Presence.

I have had the experience of becoming more acutely aware of God's presence and God's goodness in my life and in creation, most often in the fall of the year, after a most magnificent experience in nature—the quiet of the woods and colours of the trees and calmness of the lake. When we read some of Seamus Heaney's poems and reflect on some of Bruce Springsteen's music, symbols and images touching on what it is to be Catholic rise to the surface, much like pop-up ads on a computer screen. These images reflect a faith learned in childhood and a faith that continues to give meaning in adulthood. These are the Catholic elements—the images (biblical, devotional and spiritual) that helped shape the religious outlook and understanding (the imagination) of the poet and songwriter.

In the past, these Catholic elements affected children growing up in families. Children experienced values and prayer, sacraments and church liturgies, stories and activities (doing the stations of the cross, praying the family Rosary, and experiencing the liturgical seasons, such as the discipline of Lent and the joy of Easter). Children gradually acquired a Catholic imagination. (I speak here of the positive richness of the Catholic imagination existing in the pre-Vatican II church and especially celebrated since the Second Vatican Council. For some, there may still be some very negative, crippling and damaging aspects of Catholic practice based on fear and guilt experienced at times in the pre–Vatican II Catholic culture.) In the past, children were able to build on this base when they continued their education in Catholic schools. They learned the Bible lessons and the teachings of the catechism. They encountered their Catholic history and became immersed in the stories of the contributions of saints. They built on the religious and spiritual outlook that was being shaped in the family.

These Catholic elements can stay with a person; they can be indicators of something very real, which is one's faith and one's relationship with the triune God—Father, Son and Holy Spirit. These Catholic elements colour that part of the imagination that makes God real for a person, shaping the person's sense of life and understanding of eternal life, of grace and sin and forgiveness.

In the past, the family has been the key to a Catholic imagination: teaching and modelling for the young ones, sharing stories and activities, introducing children to Jesus and Mary through prayer, socializing children into the church community and helping them establish a personal relationship with God. The family—parents and grandparents—has been the key.

In parish ministry, I have often met Catholics who are experiencing a critical moment in their lives. In moments of crisis, Catholics whose liturgical or worship practice has been minimal over the years are able to fall back for meaning and support on a faith imagination shaped in their early years. The blessing is that by digging deeply into their past, they are able to recover what it is to connect with the Lord and how to go about it in prayer; they are able to express their hope and their trust. Their Catholic imagination helps them reconnect with the riches of their Catholic faith, with the roots of who they are as Christians.

These days, however, the nature of family life (when it comes to shaping a Catholic imagination) has changed dramatically. For any number of reasons, the shaping of the Catholic imagination in children in many Catholic families is not a priority. In fact, in more than a few families, this shaping activity does not exist at all. For educators charged with educating the soul, this is most unfortunate. So many children enter the Catholic school classroom with a *tabula rasa* when it comes to faith.

It should be understood that the school or the parish can in no way replicate what Catholic families in the past did instinctively in socializing their children into the faith and helping them create and own a Catholic imagination. This shaping is not the mission of the Catholic school. There is neither the time nor the privileged, intimate moments that are so important in socializing children into our faith within the family.

But I do believe that we can offer some nourishment to the faith of the young person. The starting point is to realize the importance of the imagination for one's experience of God. We can introduce the children to the Catholic elements that may help shape their religious outlook. We can help the children experience the presence of God in everyday life.

The early years—kindergarten to Grade 4—are key moments in the architecture of the Catholic imagination. A good question for the Catholic educator is "Will this young person have faith in 40 years' time, and if yes, what will that faith look like?" What can we do now that, with God's grace, may help this young person in 40 years' time to pray, have a conversation with Jesus, believe in eternal life, and awaken to the awesome reality of the Eucharist and the forgiveness of sins? I believe that it is important, even necessary, to have the intention that we are helping create and build up the Catholic imagination in the young person as we go about our faith education with these children. We must minister and teach *intentionally*.

We must also minister and teach *experientially*. The key Catholic elements are very tangible. Children develop their faith imagination by touching and feeling and hearing and seeing these Catholic things.

Frequent exploratory visits to the parish church can be a gold mine for beginning to shape a Catholic imagination. Children can experience and appreciate the following:

- the holy water and its connection with Baptism
- the sign of the cross as a mini-creed to our triune God
- the altar as the table of the Eucharistic meal and sacrifice
- God's Word, the Bible, placed on the ambo
- the sacraments of initiation and our growth into the Christian community
- the baptismal font and our birth into the Christian community
- the reserved Eucharist and the presence of Christ
- the stations of the cross and the crucifix as signs of the moment of our redemption and the forgiveness of sin
- the stations of the cross as a call to sacrifice in life
- the altar dedicated to Mary, the first disciple, as the reminder of her faith
- the idea of a genuflection as reverence
- the quiet of the church and the need for silence to go deeper into our heart in prayer
- the reconciliation room and the forgiveness of sin

The school and the classroom can be a lab to cultivate the Catholic imagination. Consider the potential effect of these initiatives:

- creating a prayer corner in the classroom and having a place of honour for the Bible, God's Word, which consoles us and challenges us
- making the Catholic school community a learning ground of communal faith
- discovering the biblical mysteries of the lives of Jesus and Mary through the Rosary
- telling the stories of the saints and situating the name of the school in our Catholic story
- appreciating the imaginative power of the crèche for the Incarnation

- reflecting on sacrifice and forgiveness—going without, giving up
- learning the liturgical seasons—Advent and Lent, Christmas and Easter, and Pentecost—that present the colours and contours of our faith

For older students, the imagination expands to privilege Catholic social teaching. Students can be given opportunities to

- learn from the poor
- participate in services based on "washing feet"
- be pro-life, holding all of life sacred from the womb to the tomb
- experience solidarity
- learn the critical dimension of faith that does justice
- appreciate that we are co-creators
- engage in pilgrimages
- serve at food banks and soup kitchens
- develop awareness of sweatshops and child labour
- learn the importance of community

Conclusion

I think a lot of what I propose may already be taking place, but I want to emphasize *the intention* of what it is that we do. We must hold that intention clearly in our teaching attitude and in our organizational strategies. The Catholic school and Catholic educators can make an enormous contribution to educating in the faith if they set out systematically and intentionally to help foster the Catholic imagination with their students. That question—"Will this young person have faith in 40 years' time, and if so, what will it look like?"—should be an abiding question in our Catholic schools. There is so much that is rich in our Catholic tradition: it can help the gift of faith within us to develop, to the point that we feel compelled to share it. Providing those learning experiences for our young students is both a gift and a privilege for Catholic education in Ontario, and a challenge for us in this exciting but uncertain postmodern culture.

REFLECTION 5

Ten Principles for the New Evangelization and Catholic Education

In the previous reflection, I proposed at some length how fostering the Catholic imagination in our students, especially in those of a very young age, can be an effective means for giving them a framework from which to relate to God and to worship and serve God as disciples of Jesus as they make their way through life. If they don't receive strong faith socialization at home, assisting them in shaping their religious imaginations with the symbols, traditions and devotions of Catholicism is a privileged way of doing evangelization in the Catholic school.

I would now like to share ten further values or principles or attitudes for evangelizing in the Catholic school that I hope can offer some nourishment for Catholic educators toiling in these challenging times. As I observed at the beginning of this journal, over the years as a teacher, faith educator, formator and pastor, I have often reflected on what an effective Catholic education looks like and how we go about doing Catholic education. I now conclude this journal and these pastoral reflections by pulling together and sharing what I feel are the key principles in promoting the new evangelization for the transmission of our faith in the Catholic education community.

In doing this, I would like to emphasize that these principles are my personal choices, and are presented in no particular order. Each principle, while theological, is also practical. My own theology of evangelization has been enriched by Bishop Claude Champagne, OMI, Bishop of Edmunston, New Brunswick, and his set of reflections on the new evangelization (2009).

1. **The goal of evangelization is to share the Good News, the person of Jesus Christ; Catholic education is at the service of the Kingdom of God.**

The mission of the church is to proclaim the person of Jesus, the Son of God, and Jesus' mission to proclaim the Kingdom of God. The mission of Catholic education is to participate fully in the mission of the church. So, Catholic education is at the service of the Kingdom of God. Now Jesus did not define what the Kingdom of God is, but he gave us lots of hints of what it is like by what he said and did:

- Jesus welcomes and integrates the marginalized in society;
- Jesus' life of prayer reveals a God of mercy and love;
- Jesus' attitude toward the law indicates that the law is not absolute—only God is absolute;
- Jesus' preaching announces pardon and mercy, not punishment; and
- Jesus changes the type of relationship among the members of the community; the dynamic among members is no longer domination.

So unless Jesus and his Kingdom are at the very core of what we are about in Catholic education, we miss the mark; we fail to realize our full potential; we are confused about who we are and what we are doing.

2. **Our starting point in evangelizing is that God loves the world.**

This reality is not always easy to feel or see, but it is the fundamental reality in which we minister and work: God loves the world.

Pope Francis says, "Before all else, the Gospel invites us to respond to the God of love who saves us, to see God in others and to go forth from ourselves to seek the good of others. Under no circumstance can this invitation be obscured" (*The Joy of the Gospel,* 39). There is a whole lot that is wrong with the world; there is much nastiness. But trumping all of that sin, evil and nastiness is the rock-solid truth that God loves the world. There is more grace in the world than evil and sin. No matter how negative and problematic the nitty-gritty becomes in the classroom or staff room or boardroom, there is always more love than evil and more reason to hope than despair. The Spirit of the Risen Christ is present in the world; the Spirit is present in the evangelizers, the witnesses in our Catholic schools; and the Spirit is present in the children, the students, those we are commissioned to accompany in the faith journey. The Spirit evangelizes. This is an essential point to remember—it is the Spirit who evangelizes, not me or you.

3. **Catholics in our schools, even the most secular or the occasional Catholics, are there *somehow* because of grace.**

I know that there are increasing numbers of non-Catholic students in our schools, but our mission is not to convert them. Mind you, collateral conversions do come about; grace works in mysterious ways, and some children and even their parents come into the church through the RCIC and RCIA as a result of the children being at the Catholic school. But historically and constitutionally, our mission is to Catholic students. The key word in this principle is *somehow.* Children are baptized; their parents place their children in a Catholic school. Maybe there is not much visible faith commitment on the part of the parents; maybe up to the moment of kindergarten, parents have not even introduced the child to Jesus or taught the child to pray. But still! The Spirit of the Risen Christ is present. Increasingly, it falls to the Catholic school community to form and accompany children in owning their Baptism and growing in their faith in Jesus and the church and forming a Catholic imagination. And it is the love and hope and faith and joy inherent in a Catholic education community that can rub off and touch the non-Catholics in our midst.

4. **"The Holy Spirit calls us to be in the middle of things as things are, not as we would like them to be."**

I love this quotation by the Irish Augustinian theologian Gabriel Daly. These are words that call us to awareness of our personal and collective vocations; that call us to a practical acceptance of our own God-given turf in which we evangelize; that assure us of the active presence of the Holy Spirit. This is a truth that we need to return to often. We are the church of now—2015 or 2016 or whenever. We are the Catholic education community of Ontario or Alberta or Saskatchewan—now. This is our reality. This is the time and place we are called to by the Holy Spirit. We are not in the 1950s or 1970s. The social and cultural settings, the route or pathway we are walking are uniquely ours. The times may be messy, but they are our times and our mess. There is no time for dramatic sighing that things should be better, or for nostalgic musings about the "good old days."

5. **We evangelize in a postmodern culture characterized by *pluralism*, with many options and choices and ways and approaches for doing things, and *ambiguity*, with much uncertainty; questions do not always have answers; we are in a time in which we must live with the questions.**

Here we deal with our particular social and cultural settings. Here we work at understanding the route or pathway we are walking. Ours is a puzzling, perplexing culture. Indeed, there are so many options, choices and possibilities. This is the tricky secular challenge. In their 2013 document *The Essential Elements of Evangelization Today,* the Canadian bishops insist that "pluralism" is the one word that sums up modern Canadian society. We live in a pluralist society where Christian faith is no longer a given. So much in this journal makes reference to that secular reality. As Christianity is now but one religion alongside many others in our society, it is not surprising that, even among Catholics, there are different ways of understanding and living and being Catholic.

There is no magic potion or proven game plan that can direct us in evangelizing in such plurality and ambiguity. There are no fail-safe how-to books. The agent for evangelization, the Catholic educator living her baptismal vocation, must begin with her own relationship with Jesus Christ. It is about being with Jesus and living with Jesus. It is her own experience of Christ that provides the strength for bold, confident witnessing to the gospel. I appreciate the words of Bishop Claude Champagne: "In our world, witnesses are needed more than teachers ... life and facts more than theory ... experience more than doctrine." In the Canadian bishops' document, *martyria* or "witness" is the first essential element proposed for evangelizing today. It follows that, in a context with a lot of plurality, there will be more than a little uncertainty and questioning. This is the ambiguity that is glued to diversity. Which is the correct choice? What is the proper approach? How do we know what to do? The economy is uncertain; the future, especially for the young, is unclear; long-standing institutions (marriage and family) that used to be points of reference for stability are changing. And questions do not always have answers. I elaborate on the context of pluralism not to say that we just accept things the way they are. I simply want to point out that this is our context; this is where the Holy Spirit wants us to do Catholic education. In all of the pluralism and in all of the ambiguity, the Holy Spirit, the Spirit of the Risen Christ, is there.

To return to the bishops' *Essential Elements* document, *koinonia* or "witness to community life" is the support that can sustain and give direction to the Catholic education community. The bishops write: "In a world wounded by division and isolation, the love lived in Christian communities to the authenticity of Jesus' mission becomes a sign of credibility of his message." Community, Christian community, is the one characteristic of Catholic education most appreciated by Catholic educators everywhere.

6. The Need for Humility: "The church is an evangelizer but begins by being evangelized itself."

Pope Paul VI wrote:

> The church is the community of believers, the community of hope lived and communicated and the community of sisterly and brotherly love, but it must always listen to what it must believe, to its reasons for hoping, and to the new commandment of love. The church is the people of God immersed in the world and often tempted by idols, and it always needs to hear anew the proclamation of the Good News which converted it to the Lord. The church has a constant need of being evangelized if it wishes to retain freshness, vigor, strength in order to proclaim the Gospel with credibility. (*On Evangelization in the Modern World*, 15)

There is a certain authenticity, freshness and power in this beautiful exhortation of Pope Paul VI from some 40 years ago. This text was quoted in preparation for the Synod on Evangelization. Pope John Paul II cited it when speaking of the new evangelization. It was referred to in the Canadian bishops' *Essential Elements* document, and mentioned frequently in Pope Francis' exhortation *On the Joy of the Gospel.* If "humility" applies to the church in its mission, it applies also to Catholic education in its mission. This is a humble theology that invites analysis, feedback and critique about the effectiveness of the church's mission, strategies, policies and structures; the same applies for Catholic education. Recently I saw it phrased this way: "Be a loving critic and a critical lover of the institutional church." And for the Catholic education community, in applying this humble theology, simply substitute "Catholic school" or "board' or "teachers' association" for "institutional church." As Catholic educators, we are all evangelizers, but we must all begin by being evangelized ourselves. This is not a one-off sort of thing; it is constant! In *The Essential Elements of Evangelization Today*, the Canadian bishops put it beautifully:

> We must have humility, because nothing is so repulsive to our contemporaries as a truth imposed by authority without the interior consent of one's conscience. We need humility because before we can even speak we must accept the other person, with his or her sufferings, criticisms and even aggression. We must listen to them with all the more attention

since the Holy Spirit is already present in them and has something to say to us. (22)

7. **The effective work of the Catholic school depends on *the quality* (defined as the joy and excitement in the ownership of one's Baptism) of the Catholic adults shaping and providing the Catholic education.**

There is a presumed understanding here that

- the school is part of a Catholic school board that privileges the Catholic character of its mission;
- Catholic education really is *educating the soul*;
- the Catholic school board, to facilitate *educating the soul,* not only values but makes possible the ongoing faith development and formation of staff as a number one priority.

This Catholic education happiness index (the joy and the excitement in the ownership of one's Baptism) refers especially to the faith commitment of the Catholic educators. Pope Francis insists that the Christian is a man or woman of joy: "When Christians have more of a sourpuss than a face that communicates the joy of being loved by God, they harm the witness of the church" (*Catholic News Service*, May 10, 2013).

How does one measure the happiness index for Catholic educators? There are some key indicators. Do they have a sense of vocation? Do they sense that they are involved in something much larger than just a school, that that they are furthering the mission of the church? Are they ready to share their faith in Jesus with their students? Do they make the effort to build a strong community as the foundation for the Catholic education project with students and parents and parish?

8. **At times, to evangelize is simply to be present, to listen.**

In reflecting on pluralism and ambiguity, which are dominant characteristics of our contemporary culture, we conclude that there is much today that cannot be easily understood. There are questions that go without answers; there are problems with no easy solutions. When it comes to serious illness or the sudden death of a loved one, what can we say? We can only be present. We can do what we can do when it comes to some of the problems and situations that some children experience at home, but often we are called simply to be there, to listen and to be present. Being present and listening are a kind of evangelization without spoken words, an evangelization replete with the interior words of prayer, prayer for the suffering and the afflicted, and prayer for ourselves for courage and strength. Being present and listening involve being faithful to the gospel project! Pope Francis says,

> We need to practice the art of listening, which is more than simply hearing. Listening in communication, is an openness of heart which makes possible that closeness without which genuine spiritual encounter cannot occur. Listening helps us find the right gesture and word which shows that we are more than simply bystanders. (*The Joy of the Gospel,* 171)

More and more, our times seem to call for the evangelization of silent presence.

9. We must take advantage of the cracks open to grace.

As Leonard Cohen puts it in "Anthem," "There is a crack in everything / That's how the light gets in." All education offers special teachable moments. In Catholic education, we experience graced moments of being there and listening and sharing faith. The death of a student, for example, is a moment of profound questioning. In the pain and confusion of the student's friends, there is an opening to grace. Eternal life takes on a more personal meaning; there is a new depth to the prayer and the cry of the heart. In this type of death, prayer is always called for, as is the expression of faith in eternal life, the belief that "life is changed, not ended"—expressed maybe in words, but for sure by action and conviction. The same can be said in the case of sickness and personal or family crisis. Celtic spirituality speaks of "the thin places," the place where or the moment when the boundaries between the divine and the human almost intermingle, moments when one can feel heaven on earth. A lively and aware inner spirit helps in discerning "the cracks" in everyday life that can be an openness for grace.

10. Priority must be given to the poor, to justice.

To do justice and to work for peace are at the very heart of a Catholic education. To do justice and to work at implementing Catholic social teaching must not only be seen—written about—but must be felt at every level of the Catholic education project in the board. The principles of Catholic social teaching, therefore, should govern the decisions and strategies made in the trustees' boardroom and senior administration planning meetings, and should shape the relationships and dealings of the Catholic school board with its employees. Pope Francis says,

> Without the preferential option for the poor, the proclamation of the Gospel, which is itself the prime form of charity, risks being misunderstood or submerged by the ocean of words which daily engulfs us in today's mass communications. (*The Joy of the Gospel,* 199)

As has been evident throughout this journal, students of all ages have hearts that are inherently open to those in need and to those who suffer because of injustice. Included in the suffering and the poor are persons yet to be born and those at the end of life who risk being abused. Catholic education for justice understands that the goods of the earth are intended for all, and that we are called to be wise caretakers of God's creation. A Catholic education shaped by justice recognizes that God has a special love for the poor, and God continually invites his church to have a preferential option for the poor. This invitation is always there for the Catholic school community as well. The ideas and strategies learned in the formal and informal curriculum of the Catholic school must be translated into concrete activity on behalf of the poor.

Doing Catholic education is a value-heavy endeavour. It concerns values for those doing Catholic education—values that are handed on and values that transform—and values for those receiving a Catholic education. There has to be an enormous bias in what we are about. If the strong bias for sharing our faith in Jesus Christ as we experience that faith in the tradition of the Catholic Church is not there on the part of parents, administrators, principals, teachers and parishes, then the entire project is on thin ice and will not succeed. One does not need to be a theologian or a mystic to do Catholic education. But one does have to be a person of faith, an owned faith. With an owned faith comes awareness: awareness of the mind and of the heart. This awareness permits us to evangelize through all of the different situations and possibilities of what constitutes a Catholic education. These ten principles for evangelizing are touchstones for the ways we can go about this sacred ministry; they are meant as helps for acquiring and maintaining that awareness of mind and heart.

> I prefer a Church which is bruised, hurting and dirty because it has been out on the streets, rather than a church which is unhealthy from being confined and from clinging to its own security. I do not want a Church concerned with being at the centre and then ends up being caught up in a web of obsessions and procedures. If something should rightly disturb us and trouble our consciences, it is the fact that so many of our brothers and sisters are living without the strength, light and consolation born of friendship with Jesus Christ, without a community of faith to support them, without meaning and a goal in life. (*The Joy of the Gospel,* 49)

A Final Word

In November 1842, Father Edward Sorin of the Congregation of Holy Cross, recently arrived from France, took ownership of 524 acres of land in northern Indiana in the United States. In January 1844, Father Sorin officially named the college he started *l'Université de Notre-Dame du Lac,* the University of Our Lady of the Lake. For the University of Notre Dame, the rest, as they say, is history.

Like Father Sorin, I am a priest religious of the Congregation of Holy Cross. I am also a graduate of the University of Notre Dame. Father Sorin's idea and ideal were to provide a college education for poor immigrant boys in the Chicago area who were, for the most part, from Ireland. Thus, the fighting Irish! Over the years, the University of Notre Dame has developed to the point where many would now consider it to be the foremost Catholic university in the United States. Certainly, college football has contributed enormously to Notre Dame's mystique. But there is so much more. Notre Dame has carefully tended to its original purpose, which is to provide a Catholic post-secondary college education.

The emphasis here is on "Catholic." The Lourdes grotto dedicated to *Notre Dame—Our Lady,* Mary, the Immaculate Conception, is a privileged holy place at the university. Notre Dame is a residence college. Each residence has a chaplain and a chapel and daily worship. The Holy Cross community continues to be an active and very visible presence at the university. Theology or religious education is among the academic requirements at Notre Dame. And more than 75 percent of the students are Catholic; they choose Notre Dame because it is a Catholic university. At Notre Dame, historical memory is very much alive. The history of the place flows easily into the present, and the history is centred on the Catholic idea and the Catholic ideal that is at the heart of the myth of Notre Dame. In being faithful to its original purpose, Notre Dame carefully nourishes and sustains its governing myth, which continues to give life to the present and direction to the future.

I propose Notre Dame as an example of myth; I elaborate on the past, present and future of myth because I feel that it is vital in understanding and maintaining our Catholic education project. I feel that "the myth of Catholic education" is real in publicly funded Catholic education. Recently, in commentaries in the secular press around court judgments and whether non-Catholic students are required to attend school liturgies and Masses, journalists would list reasons why non-Catholics attend Catholic schools in the first place. Among their reasons are these: Catholic schools tend to be superior academically, have more discipline, require uniforms, excel in sports and are centrally located. In assessing why a Catholic school might be superior to a public school, some journalists mistakenly believe that Catholic schools have smaller class sizes and a better student-to-teacher ratio. My research tells me that such is not the case. The secular commentaries miss the point regarding what makes a Catholic school different.

What a Catholic school continues to have (some more than others) is an effective governing myth that is made up of the mission to share faith in Jesus Christ, a commitment to the Catholic Christian tradition and a definite option to create an educational community that has faith in Jesus and a lived Catholicism as its glue and its purpose. This is the myth of Catholic education. These are the ideas and ideals of the past that continue to give life to the present. This myth is the unifying force in our Catholic schools, expressed in school spirit, service and outreach, and strong student–teacher relationships; it is the myth that secular commentators such as Konrad Yakabuski do not understand. Theirs is a superficial, one-dimensional understanding of Catholic education, shaped by their secular, value-free ideology, so that they fail to appreciate how this gift of Catholic education has persisted because of the enduring myth.

Of course, "a widely held but false notion" is another meaning of "myth"—the more common understanding. And this notion must serve as a constant challenge and critique to all of the partners in Catholic education. How authentic is our commitment to our mission? How does fidelity to our governing myth impact the everyday operation of any Catholic school? Are we living on the past legacy or reputation without really owning the ideals and mission and without contributing to these? In a word, are we hypocrites?

The urgency of the call to be faithful to our mission has been a leitmotif throughout this journal and these reflections. The context that frames our education is continually changing. As we have seen, the Catholic education project is being questioned, and will continue to be questioned and even attacked, by different persons and groups who see no relevance or truth in our historic claim for legitimacy. Some of the questions we must deal with are petty and vengeful. But some of the questions are indeed important; these require us to think seriously and analyze and undertake some concrete action. Indeed, we are not going to win the battle with words; we must follow through with clear action that demonstrates that the common life of Ontario or Saskatchewan or Alberta would be diminished without a publicly funded Catholic school system.

As a parish priest, I represent just one of the partners of Catholic education. I write because I feel very passionate about the publicly funded Catholic school as a grace given to us by the Lord as a place to evangelize and hand down our faith. I started this journal as something personal in which to record what exactly we do with the Catholic schools in our parish. What evangelization is taking place? How do we exploit the social capital of both parish and school? The social capital of parish for school (how the parish can assist and support the school in its mission) and school for parish (how the school enhances the life and work of the parish) need to be identified and celebrated. With our publicly funded schools, we are the most blessed of Catholic communities.

If we are faithful to our mission, but along the way lose our Catholic schools for political or economic reasons, so be it. In our fidelity to our mission, we will have done everything we were able to do. But if we should lose our Catholic schools because of complacency and indifference, because we have taken our Catholic education for granted, then we will have failed miserably. As I observed in the introduction to the journal, this would be the ultimate expression of what it is to be *dumb,* that is, to be thoughtlessly and naively careless. We will have sinned against the past, the present and the future. Historical memory of the great gift will have given way to historical amnesia. We will have betrayed our history: the passion and toil of the founders and pioneers of Catholic education. We will have dismissed our sacred duty to the present: to the thousands of young people now in our care. And we will have forfeited our evangelizing future and the great potential of sharing our faith in Jesus Christ and handing down our very rich Catholic Christian tradition.

The University of Notre Dame is dedicated to Mary, Our Lady, the Mother of God. At the conclusion of his 2013 apostolic exhortation *The Joy of the Gospel*, Pope Francis proposed that the church look to Mary as the model of evangelization. As a pastor, I conclude this lengthy reflection on the gift and challenge of Catholic education by sharing Pope Francis' most beautiful prayer to Mary as the star of the new evangelization:

Mary, Virgin and Mother,
you who, moved by the Holy Spirit,
welcomed the word of life
in the depths of your humble faith:
as you gave yourself completely to the Eternal One,
Help us to say our own "yes"
to the urgent call, as pressing as ever,
to proclaim the good news of Jesus.

Filled with Christ's presence,
You brought joy to John the Baptist,
making him exult in the womb of his mother.
Brimming over with joy,
you sang of the great things done by God.
Standing at the foot of the cross
with unyielding faith,
you received the joyful comfort of the resurrection,
and joined the disciples in awaiting the Spirit
so that the evangelizing Church might be born.

Obtain for us now a new ardour born of the resurrection,
that we may bring to all the Gospel of life
which triumphs over death.
Give us a holy courage to seek new paths,
that the gift of unfading beauty
may reach every man and woman.

Virgin of listening and contemplation,
Mother of love, Bride of the eternal wedding feast,
pray for the Church, whose pure icon you are,
that she may never be closed in on herself
or lose her passion for establishing God's kingdom.

Star of the new evangelization,
help us to bear radiant witness to communion,
service, ardent and generous faith,
justice and love of the poor,
that the joy of the Gospel
may reach to the ends of the earth,
illuminating even the fringes of our world.

Mother of the living Gospel,
wellspring of happiness for God's little ones,
pray for us.

Amen. Alleluia!